The Satisfied Customer

The Satisfied Customer

Winners and Losers in the
Battle for Buyer Preference

Claes Fornell

palgrave
macmillan

THE SATISFIED CUSTOMER
Copyright © Claes Fornell, 2007.

All rights reserved. No part of this book may be used or reproduced in any manner whatsoever without written permission except in the case of brief quotations embodied in critical articles or reviews.

First published in 2007 by
PALGRAVE MACMILLAN™
175 Fifth Avenue, New York, N.Y. 10010 and
Houndmills, Basingstoke, Hampshire, England RG21 6XS
Companies and representatives throughout the world.

PALGRAVE MACMILLAN is the global academic imprint of the Palgrave Macmillan division of St. Martin's Press, LLC and of Palgrave Macmillan Ltd. Macmillan® is a registered trademark in the United States, United Kingdom and other countries. Palgrave is a registered trademark in the European Union and other countries.

ISBN-13: 978–1–4039–8197–4
ISBN-10: 1–4039–8197–3

Library of Congress Cataloging-in-Publication Data

Fornell, Claes.
    The satisfied customer : winners and losers in the battle for buyer preference / Claes Fornell.
        p. cm.
    Includes bibliographical references and index.
    ISBN 1–4039–8197–3—ISBN 0–230–60406–4
      1. Consumer satisfaction. 2. Consumers' preferences. 3. Customer relations.
    I. Title.
HF5415.335.F67 2007
658.8'343—dc22   2007024932

A catalogue record for this book is available from the British Library.

Design by Newgen Imaging Systems (P) Ltd., Chennai, India.

First edition: December 2007

10 9 8 7 6 5 4 3 2 1

Printed in the United States of America.

Contents

Contents

List of Figures and Tables

* ACSI = American Customer Satisfaction Index

Tables

* ACSI = American Customer Satisfaction Index

CHAPTER 1

Introduction

DRIVING HOME

It was a dark and stormy night in Ann Arbor, Michigan. From the inside looking out, summer-night storms in the Midwest are often spectacular and sometimes scary. I was driving home from my office at the University of Michigan, after a long day at work a few years ago. David VanAmburg and Forrest Morgeson were busy crunching numbers for the upcoming American Customer Satisfaction Index (ACSI), to be released by mid-August 2005. The rain came in spurts, with clusters of small drops seeming to shower from the side more than from the sky. Every now and then, just as they were about to hit the ground, the rain drops seemed to merge and reverse course, going back to where they came from. The streets were nearly empty. No traffic to speak of. In a way, it was kind of nice. The cost of thinking—something economists occasionally worry about—was lower than usual because of the ease of driving. No pedestrians to worry about and hardly any other drivers out there. The ACSI data was still on my mind. What were the underlying trends in customer satisfaction? What did they mean for consumer demand, economic growth, and stock prices? What companies were in difficulty? What companies were going to benefit? And, above all, how would the new forces of the global economy impact the way we do business?

The year had not started well. Americans were getting fed up with the poor level of service; complaints were up and our customer satisfaction numbers were plunging. In the first quarter, the overall ACSI score was the worst we'd seen in 27 months. Had we reached bottom yet? Oil prices were at near record highs and real wages were falling. Households were taking on more debt and interest rates were rising. Would companies really invest more resources in beefing up customer service? The national economic outlook was full of questions—both for the long and the short term. But, as far as I was concerned, it was gratifying to see how useful the ACSI had turned out to be. The index, which we launched in 1994, had demonstrated predictive powers beyond expectations. The companies I started, CFI Group and Foresee Results, which use the same ASCI determinants to help individual companies, were doing well. After ten years, we had strong management and a cadre of very capable people. A decade of data showed that ACSI forecasts consumer spending, GDP growth, corporate earnings, and stock prices. I always thought it would do this, but the predictions were better than I had hoped for.

We were now armed with enough evidence to convince managers that it really paid off, at least in most cases, to invest in customer service improvements. But the key was not how much to invest, but *how* to make that investment and *what* to improve. Exactly what aspects of service were going to have the best economic returns? The answer, I knew, varied from company to company. I also knew how to determine what the best approach was likely to be. Much depends on the understanding of the difference between levels and changes. Most managers understand the difference between marginal cost and average cost, but when it comes to investment in customer service most managers don't think in these terms. But in just about every situation, every organization, and every task, it is the *marginal* contribution that matters most. If I push this lever, what will happen? If I change x, how will y change? The same applies to customer service and customer satisfaction. But when I discussed this with managers, their general approach was often along the lines of: "What's our service level? What do we do well? What do we do poorly? Attention would then be directed at the areas where service was considered to be poor. Now, that's not a good way to allocate scarce recourses or get the most bang for the buck.

ECONOMIC TSUNAMI

If business managers can cultivate better returns from investing in the satisfaction of their customers, investors should be able to reap similar returns by investing in businesses with these kinds of managers. As a matter of fact, the stock returns for companies that have done well on the ACSI are much better than the overall returns of the stock market. Why is this? The answer is actually quite straightforward. Investors make money from companies that increase their profits. Future profits, in a global economy where there is a lot of buyer choice, come from satisfied customers.

———

It was raining more now. Streets were overflowing; here and there it looked like mini-tsunamis—if there are such things. Similarly, it was easy enough to see that there was an economic tsunami in the making. Something so strong and so powerful that it would wipe out companies that failed to see it coming. But this also would provide a terrific opportunity. Obviously, it's not possible to surf a real tsunami. Surfing needs whitewater and breaking waves. A tsunami can be 100 miles long, but it also has an end. The economic tsunami is long too; it is generated by consumer power fused with investor capital, but it has no end in sight. There is a way to ride it—by harnessing its power for advantage rather than trying to confront it.

Because of globalization, outsourcing, information technology, and growing numbers of sellers competing for the same group of buyers, the balance of power between buyers and sellers is shifting. The implications are fundamental and far-reaching. For example, the very nature of what constitutes an economic asset is going to be very different in the future. The way we look to productivity improvements as a basis for growth will be determined, to a much greater extent, by how the buyer is affected. Otherwise, the true costs of poor service, often as a result of our push for squeezing out more productivity, will escalate to intolerable levels. And, it is the companies—not the consumers—that are going to bear the brunt of these costs. As always, however, every threat comes with an opportunity. How should business management and investors best deal with the newly empowered buyer? That's the question this book attempts to answer.

More buyer choice, more buyer information, rapid movement of capital, as well as the transferal of work across nations without transplanting labor all contribute to increased buyer power. There is no difference between the use of power in business transactions and the use of power in more general settings. Power means that you can dictate terms and make others do what they otherwise wouldn't. The more powerful the buyers, the more damage they can inflict on sellers. The punishment can be swift and brutal. Dissatisfied customers not only defect, they broadcast the seller's shortcomings in ways unimaginable only a few years ago. Gone are the days when consumers just shared their experiences with the neighbor across the fence or on the phone with a friend. In recent years we have witnessed the mushrooming of what Nielsen Buzzmetrics CMO Pete Blackshaw dubbed "consumer-generated media."[1] The Internet creates all sorts of channels for voicing opinions that can be read by millions of complete strangers via bulletin boards, chat rooms, and forums; sites specifically for customer feedback and complaints; customer reviews of products on retailers' websites; and the ever-growing number of blogs. There are an estimated 75 million blogs in cyberspace, and that number is expected to exceed 100 million by the end of 2007. Today's consumers exchange information about their purchase and consumption experiences at a breathtaking pace.[2] An offending seller will see revenues plunge, fixed costs (per unit) increase, profits deteriorate, and investor capital withdrawn. This is, of course, exactly how it should be in free markets: Sellers compete for the satisfaction of the buyer, and buyers maximize their satisfaction (or utility, to use the conventional economic term). Satisfied customers reward the seller with more business in the future, the good word spreads, and investors provide more capital to the seller. But it only works this way if the buyer is more powerful than the seller. For most of the twentieth century, that wasn't the case. Things began to change after World War II, but it's not until recently that the pace has truly accelerated.

THE BEGINNING

In 1987 I was on leave from the University of Michigan and spent half the year in France teaching at INSEAD, the international business school just outside Paris. After that, it was on to the Stockholm School of Economics. I had grown up and received my basic education in Sweden. Stockholm is my hometown and it is always nice to be back — not so much for the meatballs or the Swedish weather, but to see family and friends. Much had changed for Sweden since I lived there — perhaps the most conspicuous change, at least to an economist, had been the decline in relative wealth. From its position as one of the wealthiest countries in the world, Sweden's GDP per capita had dropped to the middle of the pack in Europe after I left for the United States in 1977. I claim no cause and effect here, but I did have some ideas on how Sweden could become a more competitive nation by better attending to the things that really mattered in the modern economy. And, more recently, the Swedish economy has done quite well.

We were having a crayfish dinner at the Stockholm Grand Hotel with representatives from the Swedish government and executives from the Royal Post Office. They wanted to discuss an idea I had presented at a seminar for improving both the way companies in Sweden did business and the competitiveness of Swedish industry. Many companies failed to prioritize customer orientation; they were more focused on labor and how to improve productivity. Swedish shipyards were the most productive in the world, but nobody bought their ships. What good is superior productivity in such a scenario?

What I had in mind was the creation of a new measure, on a nationwide basis, that could tell us more about the demand side—something about what the buyer actually experienced and, as a consequence of that experience, was likely to do in the future. In other words, what I was after was a measure of buyer utility. Such a measure should be able to tell us what companies had done to (or for) their customers. After all, consumer utility is an important standard for economic growth. But a good measure of utility—such as customer satisfaction, which is the same as "experienced utility"—should also tell us what buyers' future interactions with such companies would generally be. Would they come back and buy more? If they were satisfied, they probably would. If not, the prospects for repeat business would be less promising. This was the starting point for the Swedish Customer Satisfaction Barometer. In order to find out how satisfied customers were, we would do annual surveys, feed the data into an econometric model that would help sort out background noise and establish causes and effects, and then aggregate all these to a national number.

The government officials thought this was a great idea: "This is something we can get behind and fund." The Royal Palace, of which there was a spectacular view from the Grand Hotel, looked even better than I remembered as a kid. We had funding from the government for a new and truly exciting project. The Swedish Customer Satisfaction Barometer was not only a forerunner to the ACSI, it was also the foundation for what would become Claes Fornell International (CFI) Group, the company I founded for the purpose of helping companies strengthen their relationships with customers. As the customer satisfaction work started to take shape and get attention, I also got more of the type of phone calls that business professors typically get. The questions posed to me were of this kind: Can you help us with our company's customer satisfaction? How should we measure it? How should we get our people to embrace it? What would the financial results be? Some of these questions were reasonably straightforward to answer—especially those about measurement and the financial value of a customer. The others required more work. But what surprised me was how primitive many companies' efforts were. This was true in the United States as well as in Europe. Almost nobody used modern measurement technology. Some generated near-random numbers. Even worse, such numbers were often the basis for strategy and sometimes for executive compensation. Simplistic but all-too-common notions that the customer is always right and that customer expectations should be exceeded are not helpful. I continue to be amazed that people still believe these maxims. The same is true about the need to stay close to the customer. Sometimes, you can get too close. Customers cannot be responsible for running the business. If they were, we would soon get unsustainable cost-price ratios. Another beef of mine is the way in which companies deal with customer complaints. Most are counterproductive. For the most part, the number of complaints should be maximized. That may sound crazy, but the opportunity cost of not getting the complaint is usually much higher than the cost of dealing with the complaint in the first place. Similarly, customer loyalty is often touted as a business objective. Loyal customers are good for business, they say. But not always. It depends on the cost of getting that loyalty. And the price can be very high—just ask General Motors or Ford.

Of course, everybody knows that customers are important. Without customers, there is no revenue. Most managers understand that poor service can exact a high economic cost in competitive markets. The problem is that the total costs of unhappy customers are often underestimated. The benefits accrued from creating satisfied customers are probably even more underestimated, in part because most companies do a poor job of measuring customer satisfaction. The problems get magnified as firms face pressure to reduce costs and improve productivity. Costs are often reduced in such a way that both expenses and revenues drop—the latter usually far more than the former. This book argues that the root cause of financial failure is not managers' lack of appreciation for customers, but often the tools they employ to allocate resources for improving the value of customer assets. Developed in an era when the economy was radically different, these tools are now painfully inadequate.

I suppose my advice to companies was reasonably constructive, because the phone calls kept coming. After a while, I realized that I couldn't do all this work myself. My first step was to hire a full-time secretary to keep my schedule straight, and I asked another faculty member, Mike Ryan, to help me out. Thus the start of the CFI Group (although it had a different name in the beginning). CFI grew quickly, with clients in Europe, Asia, and the United States trying to understand, measure, and diagnose customer relationships as economic assets. Integrating financial and nonfinancial information, we were working hard to focus time, energy, and resources on the areas that most affect the economic results of our clients. The idea was that they should profit from lower customer churn, higher employee satisfaction, and higher stock prices—by learning how to invest in and grow the customer as an asset. Essentially, it comes down to being able to do the following: (1) pinpoint which aspects of the product, service, marketing, etc. have the greatest effect on customer satisfaction; (2) estimate the expected financial returns from improved satisfaction; and (3) understand what actions to take and how to best create strong customer bonds.

WHAT'S GOOD, WHAT'S BAD?

At the heart of the matter is the relationship between customer satisfaction and worker productivity and between quality and productivity.

How to best balance the two? My own feeling was that there was too much focus on productivity and that too many service companies behave as though they are manufacturers. Improving productivity isn't always for the good, even though it's almost always portrayed that way. In a way, it's strange that we have come to believe that a certain direction of change is always good or always bad. When the stock market goes up, that's good. Consumer spending is good for the economy; government spending is bad. When prices of goods go up, that's bad. On the other hand, when housing prices go up, that's good. When productivity goes up, that's good too. When interest rates go up, that's bad.

This is silly, of course. If prices go up, that's good for the seller, not for the buyer. When interest rates go up, that may be good for the lender, not for the borrower. When home prices go up, that's good for the home owner, but not for the home buyer. But why isn't productivity always good? Isn't it always desirable to be more productive? Well, it depends on what the costs are. Doing more with less, which is what productivity is, can lead to higher unemployment and less customer service. Obviously, if we fire 10 percent of our workforce and the remaining 90 percent keep production going at the same level as before, productivity has improved. But in a service economy, it is more difficult to maintain quality while producing more with fewer people. Especially when the service itself is labor intensive and requires a good deal of personal attention. In manufacturing, it is more feasible to replace labor with new technology. In order to demonstrate what the effects were, I worked with a couple of prominent researchers— Roland Rust of the University of Maryland and Eugene Anderson of the University of Michigan—to analyze data on customer service and productivity. We found that productivity and quality don't go hand in hand in the service sector.[3] This wasn't particularly surprising to us and I don't think it's contradictory to economic logic. The important thing was to demonstrate that productivity increases don't always have a positive effect. In 2006, the United States had the weakest productivity growth in 10 years and the highest customer satisfaction levels in

12 years. Coincidence? Perhaps not. Now, consider that corporate earnings were strong, inflation was in check, unemployment was low, and the stock market strong, and perhaps the notion that productivity is the key to everything good deserves a bit of rethinking.

As our research findings made their way, albeit ever so slowly, to the attention of economists, investors, and business managers, I felt pretty good driving home that night—about the ACSI and what we had accomplished. But the economy had many trouble spots. Although in recovery after the burst of the stock market bubble back in 2000, there were many concerns. My wife and I were trying to sell our house, but the housing market had slowed to a near standstill in Ann Arbor, like in many other communities across the country. Maybe it wasn't exactly the best of times or the worst of times, but we seemed to have elements of both, without either extreme claiming the upper hand.

DOUBLE WHAMMY FOR DELL

As I drove into our driveway and was about to park, Forrest, who is responsible for running the ACSI software and compiling the results, called on my car phone.

"I've got preliminary numbers for you," he said.

"Are they still going down?" I asked.

"No, they're actually up a little. Cars are doing better, e-business too. But here is something unusual," Forrest continued. "Dell is dropping like a rock."

Fortune magazine had named Dell, Inc., the most admired company in the United States only a few months earlier. Dell had steadily improved its ACSI scores, leading the PC industry until it was surpassed by Apple some five years earlier. But Apple did not compete head on with Dell and was not much of a threat.

Michael Dell had followed a very successful business model: selling directly to the user when hardly anybody else did, customizing

PCs to the needs of each individual customer, and pricing below competition. Customization is often an effective means of creating a satisfied customer. If done well, it usually leads to an ability to price above competition, but Dell's prices were also lower than most, although not all, competitors. How can you beat that? No wonder that Dell did well in the ACSI.

So, what was going on now? Why was Dell dropping in customer satisfaction? Was this just a temporary stumble or was it something more serious? Dell's stock price had not gone anywhere for some time and in the past week, the stock price had actually dropped. We had previously analyzed the relationship between Dell's ACSI movements and its stock price. The pattern was clear (even though the ACSI does not include business-to-business sales, which is the larger part of Dell's business): As customer satisfaction improved, Dell share prices tended to go up as well.

But this was a big satisfaction drop. Down by more than 5 percent (which may not seem like much, but for the ACSI, that's a lot), much below a surging Apple and close to Gateway and Hewlett Packard. Gateway, which had now also started shipping directly to customers, suffered the largest fall of all PC makers back in 2000. Serious financial difficulties followed. Was something similar going to happen to Dell?

"I think they're heading for trouble," Forrest volunteered. "There is no way they can do well financially if they drop the ball with their customers."

"What's their service score?" I asked.

"Even worse. I'm telling you, this is bad news."

It looked like one of the Dell twin engines for growth was coming off. Dell had been extremely successful and done something very few companies manage to do—combine a zeal for cost cutting with increasing customer satisfaction. But customer service is always in some degree of jeopardy if cost cutting is at the center of business strategy. It's a delicate balance, because it is always tempting to chase costs even though customer satisfaction may suffer—especially if the costs were to support service and front-line staff, or in other ways impacted the company's ability to sustain strong customer relationships. Sure enough, it now seemed that Dell had crossed the line and customer service was taking a beating.

As it turned out, this was the beginning of a huge drop in Dell's stock market value. After a little more than a year, the value of the company's stock had been cut in half. In other words, Dell had been hit by the double whammy of customer defection and capital withdrawal. When investors join customers, the power of the customer is magnified in ways that we haven't really seen before. That's not exactly the same as the Invisible Hand of Adam Smith[4]: "it is not from the benevolence of the butcher, the brewer, or the baker, that we expect our dinner, but from their regard to their own interest." The consumer wants quality at a low price. The seller wants profit. The Invisible Hand makes sure that quality goods are produced at low prices because buyers will punish sellers with low quality and/or high prices by taking their business elsewhere. Adam Smith was not talking about the movement of capital in this context. But that's what we have now. Companies with unhappy buyers will see not only their customers defect to the competition, but investment capital follow suit. Companies with increasingly satisfied customers will benefit not only from more repeat business from loyal customers, but also from an influx of capital from investors. The time it takes for investors to react varies, but there is no doubt that the reaction will be quicker in the future. As to the fortunes of Dell, the company is still being punished. It will not be easy to persuade many of the former customers to come back. But as is often the case when a company loses its focus on customer satisfaction and is punished by buyer defection and the stock market, Dell is looking to get back to the strategy that made it successful in the first place. The CEO is gone and Michael Dell himself is back at the helm. Can he meet the challenge? With customers departing and competition not only strengthening its traditional retailer focus but also copying the best aspects of Dell's business model, it's not going to be easy.

NEW RULES

Like productivity, much of what is considered "competitive strategy" is also leftover from a bygone era. The idea of beating competition as a central focus of the enterprise is going to be replaced by and become a by-product of creating a satisfied customer—or rather portfolios of satisfied customers. Downgrading or offloading service in order to beat competition on technology, price, and gadgetry, as in personal computers, cable TV, and telephone service, is not going to work. Beating competition is only worth it if there is a prize. But that prize isn't the demise of a competitor or more assets on the balance sheet, but long-term customer patronage. Satisfied customers are assets of demand, but only assets of supply get recorded on the balance sheet. Because balance sheet assets tell us less and less about the future fortunes of a company, in a buyer-driven economy, they lose much of their value, leverage, as well as profit-forecasting ability.

The principles of "winning," "beating the competition," and "improving productivity" are so ingrained in business that they are going to be difficult to dislodge, but look at what they have led to. Services, which are growing much more rapidly than manufacturing in all advanced countries and now make up the largest proportion of economic activity, are often of poor quality. As consumers become more empowered relative to sellers, this will change. In fact, we are already beginning to see changes, with companies such as Apple, Amazon, and eBay leading the way. As sellers' power weakens, they will also bear more of the cost of poor service. In a role reversal, it will be the buyer who does the "cost" cutting by not going back to the same supplier. This is different than the situation we have become used to, where the cost of poor service is largely paid for by buyers (time, effort, frustration and irritation, risk of product failure as warranty coverage shrinks, etc.).

Considering all the unabsorbed and unrecorded costs of poor service quality, there are serious macroeconomic implications as well.

While cramped airline seats, cryptic product manuals, incompetent service people, and long waits on the phone might seem like relatively minor nuisances in the greater scope of things, there are negative consequences for growth and business returns. Declining customer satisfaction reduces demand and sets in motion a vicious circle of effects that includes erosion of firms' economic value, labor uncertainty, and, ultimately, slower economic growth.

Since the costs of poor service are huge, customer dissatisfaction also represents a largely untapped profit opportunity. Firms that treat their customers well realize an advantage over their competitors, and investors that put their money into such firms reap returns that systematically outperform the stock market. The only caveat to this statement is that both product and financial markets must function reasonably well. That is, product markets must be competitive and offer buyer choice. Financial markets must be reasonably transparent and allocate capital in accordance with consumer utility. As will be demonstrated in this book, most markets are reasonably well behaved, albeit still on the slow side compared with what's to come. This book will offer insight to both the manager whose job is to allocate company resources for greater buyer preference and the shareholder/investor who judges the wisdom of that manager's effort in allocating resources.

I will also show how best to capitalize on growing consumer power for competitive advantage and superior returns. Specifically, I will talk about:

- how customer satisfaction is related to corporate earnings, market value, consumer spending, as well as GDP growth;
- why managers and investors should view satisfied customers as real economic assets;
- how understanding the causes and significance of customer satisfaction can lead not only to higher returns, but to lower decision risks and lower cost of capital;
- how to quantify—financially—the value of customer relationships, creating the Customer Asset;

- what to do and what not to do in order to reduce customer dissatis-faction and optimize satisfaction; and
- how to best apply the principles and practice of Customer Asset Management, an approach that recognizes customers for what they are: bona fide, albeit intangible, economic assets.

The way we deal with productivity, customer service, beating competition, getting close to the customer, customer complaints, and customer loyalty needs to change in order for businesses to be successful in the new era of consumer sovereignty. And it is far from certain that beating competition by preventing it from winning leads to a prize worth having. For example, if we beat competition by selling products below cost, is it worth it? Was an average discount of $3,500 worth it to General Motors to entice consumers to buy their cars?

THE INVISIBLE HAND(S)

During the first half of the twentieth century, the economy was industrial and manufacturing-oriented, and mass production was key to growth. Companies such as Ford and Coca-Cola created wealth by churning out goods for mass markets. With consumer choice limited by geographic and other boundaries, the value of a firm consisted largely of tangible assets such as factories, equipment, or real estate—all assets of supply and all measured on the balance sheet. Today, buyers have more choice and far more power to punish faltering suppliers. It is much more common for a buyer to decline an invitation to buy than it is for a seller to decline an invitation to sell. As a result, financial performance hinges less on tangible goods and assets. What really matters is the health of a firm's customer relationships. Much economic value creation today doesn't get recorded on the balance sheet. Just look at the difference between book values and market values. The market value of most service companies is much higher than the book value.

The economy has changed much more than its measurements. Measurement is still about matters of production, prices, supply, and the quantity of economic output, but the assets of production are not what they used to be. Only when buyers are weak will assets of supply be useful predictors. But by themselves, they don't tell us much about the future anymore. Unless supported by other assets, they are not as valuable, either. This is obvious once we look at the relationship between assets on the balance sheet and future income, which is getting weaker and weaker. The most essential of economic assets, when buyers are powerful, is the health and strength of the company's relationship with its customers. Since it isn't on the balance sheet, there are no standards for its measurement. But it is a powerful predictor of the future. To realize long-term gains in profit and shareholder value, managers and investors need to think of customers as investors. Like all investors, customers and employees expend resources in order to obtain a benefit with minimum risk. That is, when we buy something, we like to be reasonably certain that we'll be pleased with our purchase. We must get rid of our simplistic and one-dimensional view of productivity and make management decisions with tools that capture what's relevant and where we have leverage.

But:

- Many managers and investors still rely on traditional accounting information such as return on assets or return on investments—even though such data reflect tangible assets only.
- Managers are often pressured to cut costs where they shouldn't be cut—whether by eliminating jobs, substituting technology for labor, or reducing wages—without enough consideration given to the potentially harmful effect on customer relationships.
- For all the talk of "knowing the customer," companies still use primitive systems for measuring and analyzing intangible assets, customer satisfaction in particular. This is perplexing in view of the fact that the key to success lies in creating a satisfied customer. The only way

around that would be to create a monopoly—which is usually much more difficult to do.

At the macro level, failure of buyers and sellers to come to terms leads to economic stagnation. After all, economic growth is determined by the value of buyer-seller transactions. If such inter-actions are thwarted because the discontented buyer is unwilling to repeat a bad experience, the economy takes a hit. Economic growth, at the macro and micro level, is not just about production or supply—it is about buyers and sellers getting together and creating exchange.

We don't often speak of economic performance and customer satisfaction in the same sentence, but the relationship is all too evident. In a competitive market, satisfied customers are more likely to come back for more, while dissatisfied customers are less likely to do so. When customers don't return, potential transactions go up in smoke, leading to excess inventories and unused service capacity. Layoffs and unemployment follow, bringing about a plunge in discretionary income and consumer spending. Companies react by reducing capacity even further, and the cycle repeats itself.

"The hand of capital markets," together with "the hand of consumer markets," is creating a force strong enough to change the way business is done. It doles out reward and punishment to sellers at a much faster pace than most managers are prepared for. Due to the shifting balance of power between buyers and sellers, many companies will fail; some will prosper. Is there a way to prosper here? Standing up to power isn't going to work. How about going with the flow or trying to harness the power? What about investing? If the consumer/investor power can be harnessed, or anticipated, is there a way to make money by betting on the winners?

The answer to these questions is "yes." Because of the severity of the challenges, the opportunities are also greater than ever before. But it will require changes in how business is done today. I will explain why and how. I will also provide examples of where it works and where it doesn't.

REBATES, COST CUTTING, AND CAPITAL MOVEMENTS

"What else is going on?" I asked Forrest.

"Satisfaction with Detroit is up a little," he said.

"Really? That's good news for Michigan."

"Well, probably not, the other guys have improved even more."

The ACSI scores for U.S. cars had indeed improved, but they were falling further behind automobiles made in Japan and Korea. Rebates, low-cost financing, and employee discounts extended to the general public had led to higher sales and higher customer satisfaction for Detroit, but they had also taken a toll on profits and did not bode well for the future. By the end of 2006, over a period of less than six years, Michigan was to lose 40 percent of its auto manufacturing jobs. The rising satisfaction with Japanese and Korean cars was due not to rebates but to improvements in quality and customization. Long term, there is no question as to which strategy is better. Price promotion is a costly means for boosting customer satisfaction. If it has a positive effect at all, our data suggest that such an upsurge will be short term only. In contrast, improvements in quality tend to make a satisfied customer willing to pay more. Toyota seemed to grasp this. It had moved up to the number one spot in the ACSI and it was *raising* its prices. I knew that it was going to be very difficult for Detroit. Pleasing car buyers by lowering prices would put even more stress on margins and weaken pricing power in the future. With Detroit's high-cost structure, pricing power was critical. But without better customer satisfaction, and facing stiff competition, Detroit was stuck. What happened the following year was predictable: massive layoffs, slow sales, and no profits. The combined market value of Ford, GM, and DaimlerChrysler fell. Soon that value— of the whole U.S. automobile industry—was only a small fraction of the market value of Google, a company selling advertising space that didn't even exist until a few years ago.

If Detroit had problems, Seoul was celebrating. Hyundai, the South Korean car maker, had entered the U.S. market in the 1980s as a low-quality/low-price competitor. It was always at the very bottom in the ACSI. Poor quality, even if price is low, does not make customers happy—and it does nothing to strengthen customer relationships. The only reason anyone would buy a low-quality product is because of price, and that has more to do with one's budget limitations than one's preferences. But things changed. Hyundai improved just about everything. The improved quality was communicated by offering the best and most comprehensive warranty program the car business had ever seen. Not only did this lower the risk for buyers, it also sent a signal that the company stood resolutely behind its product. Sales soared—up 180 percent in five years. The rest of the auto industry remained flat.

"What about Hyundai?" I asked Forrest. "Are they still going gangbusters?"

"Yeah, the story of Dell and Hyundai is really the tale of two companies with a consumer revolution in the making," he replied. I was tempted to ask: "Why the Dickens did Dell let this happen?" but didn't. "Hyundai continues to do it," Forrest explained. "They are up by 4 percent—another jump like that and they will have gone from worst to best."

But it's possible that Hyundai has gone too far too fast. The improvements in car quality and customer satisfaction seem to have come at the expense of productivity. Compared with Toyota, it takes Hyundai about 66 percent more man hours to build each car.[5] That seems like too much of an imbalance between the quality-quantity forces of growth. As a result, it will be difficult for Hyundai to compete unless it gets a better grip on the satisfaction-productivity equation.

"How much does Hyundai's increased quality affect customer satisfaction and retention?" I wondered.

"Just a second, I'll take a look," Forrest said. "Well, it's actually not that much." That suggested to me that the success the company was having now might not continue. Hyundai was grabbing market share because of low price and much-improved quality, but it was still an entry-level car. For the increase in satisfaction to really pay off, the company needed a brand for the current customers to migrate to. Impressive as the Hyundai success story was, it was based on picking low-hanging fruit. The Seoul celebration was not going to last forever, and Hyundai's future was going to be more dependent on its ability to match its offerings to different segments of the buyer population and to move satisfied customers from the entry model to something else.

Dell and Hyundai are but two illustrations of the importance of balancing productivity and customer satisfaction—Dell had too much productivity at the expense of satisfaction, and Hyundai was the other way around. Not surprisingly, Dell is trying to get back to what it used to be: a leading customer satisfaction company. Hyundai is finding out that its quest for quality has had detrimental effects on cost. This is but an inkling of what the future will bring. The force will magnify: growing consumer power joined by investor capital. Capital knows no loyalty—it goes where the returns are the best. Because the balance of power between buyers and sellers is shifting in favor of the buyer, there is no mystery about which side capital is going to be on.

The new coalition between buyers and capital is not difficult to understand, but it is an unusual alliance in the sense that its members are not aware of its existence. There are no meetings, no agenda, no debates, no votes, and no legal structure. It is an invisible partnership. But there are causes and consequences. The main cause is the shift in power from sellers to buyers. The major consequence will be changes in the way we do business. The origins of buyer power can be traced to things always associated with power: choice and information. Availability of choice is power. Information is power. Today's consumer is getting more of both. Capital is attracted to the strong and tends to avoid the weak. When the strong demand satisfaction, capital makes sure that's what they get. The implication could not be clearer: Sellers that do well by their customers will be rewarded. Sellers that don't will be punished.

LOOKING FOR UNOBSERVABLES
AS 007

Upon graduation from high school and after a series of tests involving puzzle solving, combining words, seeing patterns, etc., I was assigned to the cryptology section of the Swedish army during my compulsory military service. This was a plum assignment at the Defense Department in the capital, with lunch coupons at the best restaurants in Stockholm. All the cryptologists received training in how to handle a machine gun and how to use the bayonet if the enemy came too close. I remember the first day after our training was over. As we entered the cryptology room for our daily work, we were handed our guns and ordered not to let anybody in, whether an unknown or a general. If they failed to obey us, we were told to shoot—general or no general. It didn't hurt my ego that my Swedish counterpart to a U.S. social security number is 007, which was the number by which I was addressed during my military service. Thinking back, I might have carried this too far, for too long—even today I drive an Aston Martin.

Part of our mission was to develop new ways of measuring what we couldn't see, such as the movements of unmanned Russian mini-submarines in the Baltic. At least we thought they were mini-subs, that they were unmanned, and that they were Russian.

How do you measure what you can't see?

Well, the first thing you do is figure out what, if anything, you *can* see. At the time, we were using underwater cameras to take pictures of the tracks the subs made at the bottom of the sea. The problem was that the Baltic is quite grimy in places and our photographs were not very clear. If you stare at a murky photograph long enough, you can see almost anything. But if you have many murky photographs, the problem becomes similar to puzzle solving: fitting bits and pieces of photographs together to form a coherent, meaningful whole.

Of course, it helps to know what the finished puzzle might look like. We never had an actual photograph or a picture of a real mini-sub to compare with our murky ones, but we did have some general idea what these machines might look like—like a small tank, but bigger than a modern swimming pool vacuum cleaner. In other words, we had a theory. Perhaps a bad one, but it was a start. The task then became one of arranging data, the pictures, to see if they might fit the theory.

We never did manage to arrive at a good explanation for what was going on at the bottom of the Baltic Sea, but I arrived at something else: an interest in measuring the unobservable. I've pursued this interest for over 30 years now, first as a graduate student at the University of Lund in Sweden and then as a professor at universities in Europe and the United States. As a graduate student, I studied economics and business. Although many of the concepts in economics seemed tangible enough, their empirical counterparts struck me as inherently unobservable and therefore quite resistant to quantitative measurement. Even a quantity as seemingly straightforward as "price" is not totally observable, because it has no meaning without a context. It has to refer to some notion of what one gets for the price—the quality of the object. But quality isn't available for us to touch or measure, at least not without great difficulty. In fact, the problem is considered so difficult that it seems that modern economics has more or less given up on it. Behavioral economics and psychometrics offer a way out. I was trying to blend statistics, econometrics, and psychometrics. Without getting too esoteric or getting into technical details here, I was looking for a way to marry the unobservable to the observable and then put the unobservables into cause-and-effect equations. Was there a relationship between customer satisfaction (unobservable) and stock price (observable), between customer satisfaction and market share (observable, but sometimes not easy to measure)? How about customer satisfaction and interest rates? The more I looked into this as a doctoral student at Berkeley in California and at Lund in Sweden, the more it became clear to me that there had been tremendous advancements in measurement technology in science, but it wasn't being applied in business—certainly not in the areas I was concerned with. This is still the case. Most applications within business firms use methods developed in the 1920s or earlier. Not that these methods are incorrect per se, but they are ill-suited for the task at hand. It also seems odd to think that our competence in measurement and analysis has stood still for 100 years. It hasn't. There has been great progress. The beginnings can be traced to the late nineteenth century and to the poet Carl Sandburg, but as with many of these types of measurement models, in an indirect, and probably spurious, manner.

THE SENIOR ANIMAL HUSBANDMAN

A little over 100 years ago, Carl Sandburg enrolled in Lombard College in Galesburg, Illinois, where he took a class in composition. Phillip Wright was the professor. He taught mathematics, astronomy, economics, English composition, and even physical education. Long before anybody else, Professor Wright spotted what few recognized at the time: the considerable talent of Carl Sandburg. He even published Sandburg's first collection of poetry—generally ignored by critics at the time. Though Wright sought to instill the wonder of poetry in his sons, he was disappointed that they did not show great appreciation for it. Quincy was interested in law, Theodore in engineering, and Sewall had a knack for seeing patterns that others didn't see. In 1915, Sewall became the senior animal husbandman in the U.S. Department of Agriculture, where he conducted studies of livestock inbreeding. It may seem a stretch to go from Carl Sandburg, via Phillip Wright and his son Sewall, to what I was looking for, but Sewall Wright's work on livestock inbreeding led to path analysis: a causal interpretation of correlations. There is a correlation of sorts between Carl

23

Sandburg and Sewall Wright, but it isn't causal. Sewall might have inherited his father's mathematics ability, but the correlation to Sandburg is spurious. Without a correct causal interpretation, many business managers often base decisions on correlations that turn out to be spurious. We can do so much better.

Sewall later became a distinguished professor at the University of Chicago, and received a number of honorary degrees and awards. He is the only geneticist ever to be a Fellow of the Econometric Society.

Two Swedish statisticians filled in the holes of what I needed to complete my system. In the 1970s, Karl Joreskog had developed a method for estimating causal systems, using the same principle as Wright, but now also incorporating unobservable variables. Herman Wold, who was Joreskog's dissertation chairman, came up with his own system for dealing with large systems of indirectly observed variables. I kept working on these types of systems when on the faculty at Duke and Northwestern University. Later on, at the University of Michigan, I had the good fortune of running into Fred Bookstein, a brilliant biometrician who was measuring fish bones (I have no idea why) and certain aspects of the unborn fetus. Fred introduced me to the work of Wold and I began putting things together: The resulting index of customer satisfaction could be constructed such that it would have a strong effect on consumer demand, via repeat purchases, but also provide answers to the practical question of what to do in order to optimize customer satisfaction for maximal financial return. Because we could use the system to separate the relevant from the trivial, the signal from the noise, the precision of the estimates was also improved. In a way, it allowed us to perform consumer brain surgery without a scalpel: Relying on patterns of data, we could now pinpoint how to best leverage a company's resources and get information about customers' feelings without even asking them anything about what they would like the company to do. Just like Bookstein's fish bones or fetuses, we could observe the unobservable and we could do it much better than we did looking for mini-subs in the Baltic.

THE NEW ALLIANCE: CUSTOMERS AND CAPITAL

My efforts were mostly focused on capturing the intangible nature of customer satisfaction and its implications for the firm. But there was a bigger picture here. By the late 1980s, the decline in the industrial "smokestack" economy was evident. The service sector was becoming so large that much of our economic output was—like service itself—now intangible and unobserved. Put the intangible nature of economic output together with the shift in the balance of power between buyers and sellers, and we have two of the most important characteristics of the modern economy. What's the implication for business and capital?

Power leads to more power. The capital pull from buyers is creating a new market superpower. This is not something we should fight or try to stop, because its power is too great and its force is gathering strength. Though many companies are ill prepared, there is a way to accommodate and to manage in a new reality. When the buyers are kings and investment capital fuels their power, satisfying the customer is the name of the game. It makes no sense to talk about loyalty, value, or customer recommendations in the absence of satisfaction. Hyundai is not the only company that has already picked most of the low-hanging fruit. For most companies, the easy solutions have already been implemented. We now have to go a step further. It won't be enough to react to customer changes. The key will be how well we can anticipate customer expectations and adapt to them. If we fail, the punishment will come quicker and it will be harsher than before.

The new alliance between investors and consumers has implications for the stock market and for company valuations as well. I used to wonder why professional stock pickers, on average, underperform the market. If they did no better or no worse than the market, I could understand, because that would be predicted by efficient markets theory. This theory suggests that it is impossible for anybody—no matter how smart or how dumb—to consistently beat the market—or to lose to it. But from 2000 through September 2006, over 70 percent of the actively managed large-cap funds were outpaced by the Standard & Poor's 500.[6] One may wonder why people pay for advice worse than what's available free of charge, but the reasons for the poor performance of professionals are becoming clearer to me. Robert Arnott, Chairman of Research Affiliates, an investment management firm with approximate $25 billion in assets under management, compared all major mutual funds and found that they, too, underperformed the market by an average of 3.5 percent per year. The compounded effect for even a few years translated into a large loss relative to the random stock picker. How is it that random chance, a monkey or a dart thrower, has scored a long string of victories over fund managers? There are plenty of conspiracy theories, and there might be institutional conflicts of interest at play. But it seems to me that something more fundamental is also of relevance: a systemic distortion of information.

One need not look hard to discover regular distortions. Because companies' most relevant assets aren't reported on the balance sheet, accounting doesn't recognize investments in customer assets; companies are therefore forced to expense them. But if we invest in, say, the training of staff in order to improve customer service, the financial benefits of such training accrue in the future. The mismatch violates a basic accounting principle: The correspondence and timing of expenses and revenue. It also leads to more short-term pressure on the firm and, in the words of New York University accounting Professor Baruch Lev, a misleading picture of how the firm makes money. Under current accounting practices, investors see only part of the picture— the cost and revenue changes. They don't see the changes in the customer asset, which are critical to long-term growth.

Where would you rather put your money: In a firm that reports a large increase in quarterly profits, but whose customer satisfaction levels were falling, or in a firm that reports a large drop in quarterly profits, but whose satisfaction levels were sharply rising? The likely answer is firm number two—although you'd never know that merely by looking at public documents. The first firm is eroding its capability to make money in the future by weakening its customer asset; its current profit increase is probably a short-term result of reductions in customer service. Firm number two, on the other hand, is strengthening its relationship with customers; its reduction in short-term profit is likely due to investments the firm is making to upgrade service (e.g., staff training, new hires, etc.).

I make this assertion because I have yet to lose to the market in any year and the explanation for it lies in understanding the major forces that drive future net cash flows: the strength of customer relationships. Armed with knowledge about these relationships, my stock portfolio has returned about 100 percentage points more than the Standard & Poor's 500 over the past five years.

STRUCTURE OF THE BOOK

Before getting to issues of management, it is important to understand the broader context. I will begin by sketching the big picture—the macroeconomy and what drives it. Next I will explore what makes economies grow, the dangers of too much productivity, what determines consumer spending, and the global forces behind consumer empowerment. I will also address the most basic of all questions in business—how to make money. The key, as I see it, is to realize that economic assets are not what they used to be and the ones we really need to understand are not the ones accountants keep track of. Financial success will come to those who realize that the modern economy is less about productive resources than it is about economic relationships. The American consumer depends on financing outside the United States—mostly from China and Japan. The Japanese and Chinese consumer is hedging against whatever hardship the future might bring and spends far less than earned. Americans spend more than they earn. China cannot get rid of its enormous dollar holdings without hurting both its exports and the value of its capital reserve. A shrinking number of firms can stay in business without catering to consumer demands. Those with the healthiest customer relationships are usually the ones that do best financially. And, this will become even more so in the future.

Then, I will turn to the question of what business managers need to know and what they should do when dealing with powerful customers supported by investors' movement of capital. The perspective will be somewhat different from most business books. I believe that a scientific approach is better than relying on instincts, no matter how distinguished—not in every context or situation, but in most of them. That doesn't mean that intuition, experience, or educated guesses don't play a role. They play a big role, but shouldn't replace disciplined thinking, which is the hallmark of the scientific approach. Readers who don't find science particularly endearing should not fret. This stuff is not as difficult as it may seem—certainly not in this book.

I will touch on neuroscience, quantum mechanics, and classical economics. For example, most advanced economies have gone from agriculture to service and information via manufacturing. Service is, by definition, intangible. As a result, a growing part of the economy is not directly observable to us. The most important economic assets are not observable either. Adam Smith's Invisible Hand was obviously not observed. Otherwise, he would have called it something else. The same is true for the Invisible Hands. Consumer markets are represented by one "hand" and equity markets by another. These are the hands that spank bad companies and reward good ones. Not only can we not see this disciplinary force, or much of what we produce in the economy, but we cannot even observe the power behind the force itself: consumer utility. One cannot see the extent to which customers are satisfied. We can ask them, we can hear them growl or see them smile, but we can't actually observe their satisfaction or dissatisfaction, directly. Uncomfortable to some, the fact is that we live in an intangible economy and our recording systems regarding intangibles is primitive. Much of what we do, record, and measure is rooted in an economy that no longer exists. But there are ways to capture and measure that which we can't see. And there are ways to connect the intangible to the tangible. This is the key. Unless intangible assets, intangible powers, and intangible utility can be connected to tangible profits, we will not make much progress.

Let's start with the big picture. What's the impact of the global economy? It is changing the way business is done. What would it take for a business to do well? Understanding where the real assets are. What has changed and what hasn't? Why do we think that rising productivity is always for the good? In the new economy, it isn't. Why do we think that progress is accelerating? It's slowing. What's the new theory of growth? It's no longer about capital and real estate. What's wrong with accounting? It doesn't report on what's relevant. Why do professional stock pickers do so poorly? Who knows, but it's a fact. Who has done well in forging strong customer relationships? Who hasn't? What lessons can be drawn? What happened to the share prices of the companies that have high and low customer satisfaction? What's the implication for the business manager and for the investor?

I will attempt to clarify a host of myths and misunderstandings about customer satisfaction, market share, customer loyalty, customer recommendations, and customer complaints. From simple economic analysis, some popular business practices will be shown to be counterproductive—producing results in exact opposition of what they are supposed to. A better way would be to view the value of the size and strength of customer relationships as the *sum* of all company assets. Unless an asset contributes to the customer asset, in one way or another, it has no value. Most of what we do in management and as consumers can be viewed from an investment perspective. It can be long term or short term. The point is that we can view customers as investments. *And* we can also view them as investors. If we do, we're in the business of helping our customers manage their investments, not as a brokerage firm would but in allocation of resources such as their time, effort, and money. Everybody—customers, employees, traders, parents, spouses, etc.—is an investor. We all expend resources in order to get something. Companies that help their customers manage their resources well are likely to be rewarded. Companies that follow the tradition of off-loading work onto their customers will face difficulties.

Dissatisfaction with poor service exacts a measurable toll on business. According to our estimates, a one-percentage drop in customer satisfaction has cost the average company in the ACSI index slightly more than one billion dollars.[7] Companies with low customer satisfaction have also fared much worse in the stock market than those with high satisfaction. The underlying reason is easy to understand: Long-term profits come from satisfied customers. If customers aren't satisfied, they will, if given a choice, hesitate to patronize the same supplier again, unless persuaded by a better price. If managers calculated the value of the customer asset, they would achieve a far better understanding of the relationship between the firm's current condition and its future capacity to produce wealth. This in turn would allow managers to leverage the firm's customer asset for higher levels of net cash flows with less volatility. In other words, by following the principles of Customer Asset Management, we would be much more likely to generate high returns and lower risk at the same time. This might sound contradictory to standard thinking, but it's a logical conclusion from having highly satisfied customers: We can depend on them and they can depend on us. It would be risky for us to lose their trust. It would be risky for them to try another supplier.

CHAPTER 2

The Big Picture

HOW TO MAKE MONEY

On the first day of class, I would ask my MBA students why they decided to go to business school. The answers have varied somewhat over the past 20 years or so, ranging from "I want to have a good career" to "I want to learn how to make money." Many MBA students have broader aspirations as well, but we are talking about students of business here. Most of them go to business school because they want to know how to manage people and money. I then try to conceal whatever I might know about the topic behind the business school Socratic teaching practice and throw the question back to the students: "Well, how *do* you make money? The reply is usually some variant of "buying cheap and selling dear."

Correct, but not very useful. No extra points.

The students quickly recognize this, of course, and move on to arguments about creating something for which there is a great market need. But, again, their responses are devoid of any practical guidance on what one should actually do. After a while, the discussion ends where it began—nowhere. At that point, it seems okay to pause, take a step back, and suggest that we go back to the basics of basics. What's the elementary issue here? Doing well in the future. How should we act today in order to be better off tomorrow? A good deal of the answer lies in our ability to see what's coming—to predict or influence the future. Our survival has always depended on this—whether we are talking about global warming or finding shelter. Ancient man was better at this than his competition. We learned to stay away from the Sabertooth tiger, trap the wild pig, catch fish, use fire, etc.

Today, the objects have changed, but the principle of foresight hasn't. The better our predictions, the greater our chances for a better tomorrow. People who predict well usually end up in a more favorable circumstance than those who don't. Those who predicted that the stock price of, say, DirecTv, the VF Corporation, Northeast Utilities, Kohl's, and J.C. Penney would go up in 2006 made good money. The average stock price gain for these companies was 52 percent. With the possible exception of DirecTv, they are not companies typically associated with the high flyers of the stock market or risky bets. So, what did they have in common? Strong and growing customer satisfaction, that's what! A satisfied customer tends to recompense the seller with more business at a steady pace. The result is higher levels of net cash flows *and* lower volatility. Assuming that we knew that these companies had strong customer satisfaction, this is an example of predicting by cause-and-effect inference. But I am still talking about probabilities. Nothing is certain and it isn't always true that satisfied customers come back for more. But it's usually true. Obviously, I would be even better off if I could pinpoint the circumstances under which it wasn't true, but accurate predictions don't always imply that we understand what's going on.

On the corner of State and Oakbrook, a block from my office, there's a traffic light. Here, I make daily predictions about the relationship between the movement of cars and the color of the light. When the light turns red, my forecast accuracy that an approaching car will stop is 100 percent. I have never been wrong. As a result, I am still alive and I usually make it home for dinner. I understand why the cars stop, but I don't need to know in order to predict well in this case.

Another useful forecast concerns my shoes: In the morning when I put them on, I predict that they will remain attached to my feet for the remainder of the day. In this case, I perform a function y with the effect x. The cost of being wrong is less than in the traffic light situation, but again, my forecasts are always right on. I make hundreds of similar forecasts every day. Most turn out to be accurate. Admittedly, I am not alone in having this ability and that's a good thing, too. My predictions depend on a certain order and organization of how others behave. People sometimes say that the future is unpredictable. That's not exactly true. Most of the future is highly predictable for most of us most of the time. If it wasn't, we would have gone extinct long ago. The majority of tomorrows are not that much different from most yesterdays. Boring perhaps, but necessary for our continued existence.

Although the reasons for human forecasting prowess might be obvious, let's make sure we nail down what's going on here. What do we need in order to predict the future? One of two conditions, and sometimes both, are required. One is chronological observation. If I observe the same sequence or pattern repeating itself over a long period of time—car approaching, traffic light turning red, car stopping—I can be pretty sure that the pattern will remain in the future. There is no need to understand what I observe here. A Martian, without knowledge of our traffic laws, would make the same forecast. I don't need to know anything about the underlying causes that make cars stop at a red light. My predictions will be okay anyway. There is a bit more cause-and-effect expertise involved in tying one's shoes because there is a certain skill involved in the tying process. If the knot is too loose or the shoe strings frayed, things may not work out the way one intended. This is all trivial, one might object, but that's the point. In order to uncover what's really going on, it is helpful to understand that things are not always what they seem. We all benefit from sharing knowledge, but in a competitive situation, I am much better off knowing something others don't. Now, this is the knowledge that is valuable for management decisions in general and investment decisions in particular.

HAZARDS OF THE OBVIOUS

Extrapolating a prediction from one circumstance to another isn't always wise and here we usually need more than observation. Science talks about the interplay between data and theory. What this means is that we sometimes need to understand what we observe in order to make good predictions. Let's go back to the traffic example. I grew up in an environment where there were harsh social and legal penalties for running a red light and hitting a pedestrian. If a pedestrian put a foot on the street, whether or not there was a marked crossing, oncoming cars would definitely stop. Not so in Shanghai, Paris, or Mexico City, as I have found out. It's not simply that there's a lot of traffic in these cities, but in Shanghai, for example, there's also an assortment of cars, motor bikes, and bicycles all moving without the assistance of linearity or discernible lanes. Even at a red light, an unknown fraction of cars, and precisely zero bikers, actually stop. Cars turning right into pedestrian crossings definitely don't. After a series of near misses, I asked Yifan Tang, the head of our offices in China, why it was that the turning drivers behaved as if they had the right of way. The reason was simple. They had the right of way. Why was this? It's all about power, Yifan explained. Not long ago, only the powerful drove cars in China. The pedestrians were, well, pedestrians. This hasn't changed. What has changed is that there are more cars. The new drivers have simply assumed the same powers as the drivers before them.

All business books, in one way or another, talk about predicting the future. All management and investment decisions are about relating today to the future: how to influence it, how to benefit from it, how to defend against it, and how to adapt to it. Although most of our everyday forecasting is easy and second nature to anyone with ordinary powers of observation and recall, the deviations from one situation to another are what trip us up. Here, empirical observation isn't enough. Some form of understanding about the forces that shape future events is needed. And, the most valuable predictions depend on seeing what others don't—or the contrary to what appears to be true. Here is where value is created and where fortunes are made.

There is no doubt that the combination of systematic thinking, often with the help of economic or statistical theory, and methodical observation can either uncover the "unobservable" or prove conventional wisdom erroneous. In their best-selling book, *Freakonomics*, Steven Levitt and Stephen Dubner[1] used probability theory to analyze data about sumo wrestlers and school teachers and found that both cheat. A significant number of sumo wrestlers rig matches (in a quid pro quo arrangement with their opponents) and some teachers provide correct answers to multiple choice exams (to demonstrate that their students had been well taught). Although not without controversy about method, Levitt and Dubner also showed that abortions reduce future crime and swimming pools are more life-threatening than guns. Once we think about it, it may seem plausible and it might even be obvious, but that's in hindsight—and not until we put swimming pools and guns into the same context.

There are many situations in which the "obvious" is not at all obvious and in fact is in exact opposition to reality. For example, consider the case of bicycle helmets. Most people probably think that putting on a helmet makes cyclists safer, which is presumably why helmets are getting more popular. But is it true? Are you safer wearing a helmet? The answer to that question depends on the extent to which, if any, your wearing a helmet changes behaviors—yours and/or those of motorists. It's conceivable, I suppose, that cyclists donning protective head gear might compensate by taking greater traffic risks. It's also possible that the behavior of motorists is affected. According to Ian Walker,[2] a researcher at the University of Bath in England, there is no support for the notion that people with helmets become daredevils, but the latter is true. In a systematic experiment, he found that passing cars came on average 3.35 inches closer when he was wearing a helmet. Some came a lot closer. If wearing helmets changes the behavior of drivers for the worse, the cyclist's risk of getting hit has increased—with a potentially higher risk of injury. It's not totally clear exactly why this happens, but it's possible that car drivers look upon helmets as an indication that the cyclist in question is more experienced and can therefore be passed with less caution.[3] Obviously, when there is general agreement about what's obvious even though reality is the exact opposite, opportunities abound for those who look beneath the surface and apply a bit more logic to perception.

WHY IS TIME GOING FASTER TODAY?

As the effect of wearing a bicycle helmet or driving patterns in Shanghai suggest, it may be useful to know *why* things happen—not merely *that* they happen. But even the basic feature of the future, and the past for that matter—the passing of time—is tricky. It was a little over 100 years ago (in 1905) that Albert Einstein showed that time was not absolute, independent of other things. We also know that perception of time is affected by context. For example, it is well known that time seems to go faster as we get older. While not part of relativity theory, the explanation is in our frame of reference. Two years is only 4 percent of a 50-year-old's life. To a toddler of four years, it is 50 percent. But this doesn't totally explain why most people think that time is going faster now and why they think that things change more rapidly. Some claim that much of what we teach at the university level will be obsolete by the time our students graduate. There's just too much change. In our executive programs at the University of Michigan, we adapt by persuading former students to go back to school. Education is a lifelong quest. And while that pursuit pays the instructor's salary, obsolescence is what we all want to avoid.

If things truly are changing at a faster rate today, if the rate of change in the world around us is accelerating, and the risk of being replaced by something new is more prevalent, the implications for the way we live, how we cope, and how we do business are going to be huge. But is knowledge obsolescence on the rise? Does time go faster now? How about the need to adapt to or deal with changing circumstances? Aren't we all getting more harried? Probably, but it's not because things are changing more than before. True, we have instant communications, there are 24-hour news broadcasts, all kinds of transactions can be conducted in a matter of seconds (well, perhaps minutes) over the Internet, and the movement of money can certainly be quick. Technological progress, from communications to "just in time" inventory to delivery systems to Six Sigma, has led to higher productivity, but the benefits of that productivity have not freed us to do less work. We work more hours now—especially in the United States, though Europe is moving in the same direction. For most people, the cost of time is increasing at an accelerating rate. This too has important implications. For example, the 100-year-old business practice of off-loading work on customers will begin to be reversed: Companies will do what consumers used to do. That is, doctors will make more house calls, grocery stores will deliver to the home, companies will package birthday gifts, etc. Hmm, haven't we been here before? The economic question is about the extent to which time is becoming an increasingly scarce resource and if so, what do we do about it. But this is different than coping with rapidly changing circumstances.

Compared with the tumultuous changes our grandparents or great grandparents faced, modern life seems positively dull. It doesn't come close to presenting the type of challenges faced by some earlier generations. If anybody is in doubt, it's useful to construct a conceptual time machine. Since there is no need to travel into the future for the proper perspective here, this is not going to be difficult. All that's required is a bit of twentieth-century history. Let's invite a few friends to travel some 50 to 55 years back in time and then make a second stop 100 years back in time.

Everything gets more complicated when time and space collide, so let's limit our experiment to one variable—time—and constrain the space to either North America or Western Europe. Now then, let's turn the time dial on our imaginary machine and disembark in the mid 1950s. Have we arrived in a strange place? Can we survive? Actually, some of us have been here before. And even to those of us who were born later, the 1950s would not be an unfamiliar place. People had running water, bathrooms, and water toilets. Cars were common. There were electric lights, heating, dryers, laundry machines, radio and television, vacuum cleaners, telephones, tape recorders, newspaper delivery, air conditioning, coffee filters, supermarkets, computers (big ones), parking meters, beer cans, airplanes, and traffic lights. Dad worked at the office; mom at home. There were movie theaters, movie stars, and rock stars. Some of our time travelers might miss their cell phones, PCs, or digital cameras, but their adjustment to life in the 1950s would not be too difficult. Some might even wonder if there has been progress at all. Where are the twenty-first century's counterparts to Brando, Churchill, Einstein, Elvis, Picasso, Sartre, Ben-Gurion, and the Quarrymen?

But the structure of business was dramatically different in the 1950s. This is most evident in the United States. On March 1, 1957, the Standard & Poor's 500 stock index was introduced. Even though the index was initially composed of 500 firms, almost 1,000 new companies have been added, as others have been deleted, since then. Today, the technology, health care, and financial sectors make up almost 50 percent of the index. In 1957, they comprised a mere 6 percent. Materials and energy, on the other hand, originally made up 50 percent—now they are only 12 percent.[4]

Agreeable as it might be, our visit to the 1950s is short as we make an interim stop to pick up more travelers. Now, let's imagine that we take on a group of high school students and some recent college graduates and travel another 50 years back in time to the beginning of the twentieth century. Now, this is an alien place—not only to the time travelers from the twenty-first century, but to our passengers from the 1950s as well. No electricity, no indoor plumbing, no television, no radio, no cars, no telephones, no air conditioning, and no fast food. But a lot of horse manure on the streets. We can go on and on about what we would be missing. The people of 1900 look strange, too. The need to adapt would be a lot greater for the 1950s family traveling to 1900 than for today's family traveling to the 1950s.

In other words, the rate of change has not accelerated but slowed down since then.[5] But the effect of globalization and consumer empowerment make time go faster. There are more workers competing for jobs and more companies competing for customers. The result is shortage of time. Time goes faster because there is less of it. Not because we are faced with tremendous changes in our everyday lives. The powerful consumer continually demands, and gets, more. If not, she takes her business elsewhere. Whatever productivity gains the communications/technological revolution has brought about cannot be converted into leisure when buyers are calling the shots—they are put back into the production process. Otherwise, we can't stay competitive. Americans are now working many more hours than people in most other countries. They are also working more hours than before. It's not unusual to spend 12 hours at the office, jump on a plane, have a business dinner, and then rise early the next day in order to talk to customers in a European time zone. It seems that, for some people, 18-hour workdays are becoming the norm. Saturdays have once again become work days for many. Because buyers are getting more powerful, competition for buyers is intensifying and many workers have become increasingly replaceable. It's not because Americans put less value on leisure time, as is often said, but because they generally don't have much of a choice. Labor mobility is high but the cost of worker replacement is not. Time is of the essence—we have too little of it. Even seconds count. The time difference between using a rotary phone compared to a cell phone is 11 seconds,[6] but such a delay seems like an eternity to many people. The perception of time has important implications for business as well.

Disney tries to manage time better for its guests by using "fast lanes" and entertainment for people in line. Hotels are implementing high-tech queuing techniques for their elevators. Because of its scarcity, we are placing a premium on time and we would like to have greater control over how it is applied. But since we actually have less control, there will be an increasing demand for help in allocating time. Home shopping will continue to grow. Home delivery will make a return. Demand for fast food will continue to grow. We will see more take-out food, more housecleaning services and yard services, and less "do-it-yourself." We will be prepared to pay more for services that buy us additional discretionary time. Business will respond. A food manufacturer like Kraft provides consumers with time-saving recipes featuring Kraft foods among their ingredients. Pick up any jar of Kraft mayonnaise and you're are likely to find a recipe or meal idea. So, too, a can of Campbell's soup often displays a recipe on its label. Costco, the largest membership wholesale warehouse club in the United States, supplies time by limiting (!) consumer choice. Its more than 500 warehouses offer discount prices on a wide range of products, including computer hardware and software, pharmaceuticals, tires, and food. Costco relies heavily on repeat business and volume. Its prices are very close to cost. One key to both low cost and high customer satisfaction lies in the company's product selection. A Costco store carries about 4,000 products. By comparison, a Kmart carries 40,000–60,000. If Costco's product selections correspond well to buyer preferences, buyers benefit from having the best-value brands stocked. They also save time and effort that would otherwise be required for comparison shopping.

Workers are the losers in the global economy thus far—not just blue-collar workers, but everybody whose job can be done by somebody else—whether that person is in the United States, Europe, Asia, or Latin America. In the United States, the effects of the new job mobility are evident in the wage stagnation. Except for a short period in the late 1990s, there have been no pay increases to speak of. Adjusted for inflation, hourly wages are actually about 10 percent lower than they were in the early 1970s.[7]

It is difficult to see how the developing scarcity of time can be reversed in a free market economy. No country will be immune to the pressures of serving the customer better. The old saying that "if you don't take care of your customer, somebody else will," will take on greater importance. I am not suggesting that this is good or bad, but increasing consumer power doesn't come without sacrifice. Thus far, workers have been bearing the most of these costs. The owners of capital have not. In fact, return on capital has grown, while return on labor has plunged. The proportion of national capital in the Unites States that goes to workers is declining even though workers put in more hours. But capital does what it always does: It aligns with power. Since power is being transferred to consumers, we will see a new alliance— between consumers and capital.

PRODUCTIVITY—NOT ALWAYS FOR THE GOOD

Whenever there is a discussion about economic growth, it usually involves productivity. If we become more productive, the economy will grow and produce all sorts of benefits, chief among them rising incomes, a better standard of living, and, yes, more customer satisfaction. But productivity is not quite that straightforward. One misconception is that U.S. productivity growth leads the world. Since 1950, however, Europe has done better. Its productivity growth has averaged 3.3 percent, much higher than the 2 percent recorded in the United States.[8] Yet, GDP per capita is considerably higher in the United States. To some extent, this reflects some quirks in the GDP measure itself. (The U.S. GDP is boosted by higher crime rates, the incarceration of a high proportion of its population, and longer working hours, for example). But although there seems to have been more incremental, as opposed to breakthrough, progress during the most recent 50 years, some things have changed dramatically—especially in business. As a result of the shift in economic activity from manufacturing toward service and information exchange, the modern economy is very different from the one around which most economic theory and measurement was developed. It is also very different from the economy around which most economic theory, accounting, and management practices were developed. Economic progress, for firms and for nations, is no longer simply a matter of producing more with fewer resources (i.e., productivity), but rather a matter of better matching supply to a progressively heterogeneous demand. Yet, poor productivity is a common scapegoat for weak growth. To some extent, bizarre as it may sound to some, there is reason to suspect that it might be the other way around. The problem is that improved productivity doesn't always lead to better quality, higher consumer utility, or better living standards. This is evident in the service sector, but even in manufacturing, it is by no means apparent that productivity growth due to closing plants and laying off workers is all for the better.

Living standards and economic growth depend on the productivity of economic resources as well as the quality of output that those resources generate. Under these circumstances, does it always make sense to pursue both productivity and customer satisfaction? Isn't there some tradeoff here? The businesses of Wal-Mart and McDonald's are much more geared toward productivity than superiority in customer satisfaction. Both companies would probably gain from improving their customer satisfaction, but not as much as, say, Google would lose if its customers became less enamored with its services. There is always some balance between customer satisfaction and productivity and that balance is different for different companies. Nevertheless, there is widespread belief that excelling at both should be a general business priority. But clearly, the two aren't always compatible. If a firm downsizes, productivity (e.g., sales per employee) may increase in the short term, but future profitability will be mortgaged if customer satisfaction is dependent on the service provided by the sales staff.

Productivity gains are usually reported as good news for the economy and good news for the company, but just like good and bad cholesterol, there is good and bad productivity. What happens when we have fewer doctors per patient, fewer waiters per table, and more students per teacher? Productivity goes up, but is quality better? Are customers more satisfied? How do you improve the productivity of a symphony orchestra? Have it play faster? But how about substituting labor for technology? At the Brooklyn Opera Company, *The Marriage of Figaro* was performed by no more than 12 musicians. Computers replaced the others. It's more productive, but is it better? Replace the remaining 12 musicians and productivity goes up again. And we could go on and on. In the end, we will all stay at home and listen to CDs.

The fact is that large increases in productivity can have adverse effects, particularly in a service economy. It is the same as any other difference between quantity and quality. The idea of productivity as the ultimate driver of economic health is rooted in smokestack economics and in the assumption that prices would adequately reflect differences in quality, but the role of productivity in the service/information economy is more complicated. Like cholesterol, it is about lowering "bad" productivity while bolstering the "good."

CUSTOMERS AS ECONOMIC ASSETS

In terms of money spent, consumer service consumption in the United States is now twice the size of manufacturing. In 1950, it was the exact opposite. The implications are great—much greater than is generally recognized. It has, for one, made much of our accounting system obsolete. Larry Selden and Geoffrey Colvin discussed a company that acquires 5,000 new customers at a marketing/selling cost of $1,000 per customer. It's typical for this company to keep customers for about three years and each customer nets $300 in profit per year. Obviously, this is a losing proposition. The cost of getting a customer is higher than the income generated. But that's not necessarily the picture painted by accounting. In the first year, the results are clear enough. 5,000 customers at $1,000 each amount to an acquisition cost of $5 million. These customers generate a net income of $300 each for a total of $1.5 million. Thus, there's a loss of $3.5 million. But look what happens next year. 1,000 additional customers were acquired at the same cost. That's a total of $1 million. Now then, there are 6,000 customers cach generating a net income to the company of $300 each, for a total of $1.8 million. Since the cost this year was $1 million, profit was $800,000. If the company adds another 1,000 customers next year, it makes even more profit.

Each customer is actually unprofitable and the more customers the company gets, the more economic value it destroys. But accounting tells a different story: a healthy company with rapidly growing profits—fooling managers and investors alike. Selden and Colvin go on to explain that this situation cannot go on forever and point to the deception of averages (each customer is assumed to be economically the same), but there is an even more obvious problem here. The assets that create growth are not recognized. Unlike plants, equipment, real estate, and inventory, customer assets are not included in the balance sheet. Customer acquisition is considered a cost, not an investment. This is what's causing the distortion. It's also violating a fundamental accounting principle: matching revenues and cost. By treating customers as cost without capitalizing over time, the accounting numbers become nonsensical. So why aren't companies changing their ways here? For one thing, it would probably be against the law in most countries. If an asset isn't recognized in the balance sheet, it cannot be capitalized over time. But that's a weak defense.

Some ten years ago, AOL showed the way. Its customer acquisition costs were capitalized with the argument that the expenditure created a stream of future income. Despite the fact that this made a good deal of sense and that the argument was cogent, AOL was forced to go back to the old ways and eventually expensed its whole customer acquisition costs—thereby exaggerating costs in early time periods and profits in later ones.

If you want to make a reservation at El Bulli, a restaurant about 100 miles outside Barcelona, at Fat Duck in Berkshire, or at Nobu in London, you'll find that it's very difficult to get a table. Elite restaurants are getting smaller and there is real competition among diners to get in. Along with a few other industries, especially energy, these are the exceptions to the rule. Virtually everywhere else, the balance of power between buyer and seller is shifting toward the buyer. *The Economist*[9] describes the "all-seeing, all-knowing" consumer and states that the new consumer power is changing the way the world shops. The ability to get information about whatever you want, at any time you want, has also led to huge increases of consumer choice alternatives. The implications for business are enormous. Threatening to most, welcome to a few. Who would want to lose power? But it's a given! Buyers hold the cards. The question is what to do, given that reality. As Internet search firms offer more localized services, purchase alternatives will become even more abundant. At an instant, anybody with a mobile phone will be able to find a local store and compare prices without much effort.

The proliferation of Internet use has coincided, and to some extent caused, global competition and a global division of labor. Sellers compete harder for buyer preference. As a result, we need performance measures from the buying side, external to production. It doesn't matter how much a company can increase the quality of its products and services, unless the satisfaction of its customers is also increased. Information about customer satisfaction tells us what the company *has done* to its customers. This is the "new accounting." It's relevant because it says something about the company's current condition. But even more important, information about the satisfaction of a company's customers also tells us something about the future. Specifically, it tells us what the customers *will do* to the company. Will they come back? Will they defect? How sensitive would they be to price hikes? And this, of course, relates to the company's future capacity to produce wealth.

Satisfied customers represent a real, albeit intangible, economic asset. An economic asset generates future income streams for the owner of that asset. If it doesn't do this, it has no value and it's not an asset.

Peter Drucker said it best many years ago: "The purpose of business is to create a satisfied customer."[10] This is one of the most fundamental principles upon which a free market depends: Sellers compete for buyers. It is what makes the economy grow, what makes things better. It is the satisfaction of its customers that brings financial rewards to the firm—from customers and investors alike. Likewise, dissatisfied customers punish sellers by taking their business elsewhere. In a service economy with growing consumer power, the traditional assets of supply don't tell us much about the future. It is much more common for a buyer to reject an invitation to buy than it is for a seller to decline to sell; yet most measures about our economy and about companies continue to be supply oriented rather than demand focused.

The business imperative for creating a satisfied customer is as old as business itself. But so is the practice of taking the customer for granted with little regard for quality and service. How it comes out depends on who can dictate terms and who can walk away. It's about power. When buyers have it, sellers try to please them. In a free market, there is a mutually beneficial proposition from increasing customer satisfaction: Sellers make more profit and buyers are better off. Sellers maximize profits and buyers maximize utility. If sellers don't benefit by satisfying the customer, something is amiss—the market is not working as it is supposed to. If sellers make profits without satisfying the customer, the conclusion is the same. The market is not working properly. Most markets in most developed countries work reasonably well. But there are those that don't. In the cable TV industry, Comcast's customers are not very satisfied. In fact, Comcast is one of the lowest-scoring companies in the ACSI. As customer satisfaction plunged, revenues increased. Net income surged by 175 percent and its stock price climbed by almost 50 percent in 2006–2007.

The extent to which buyers financially reward sellers that satisfy them and punish those that don't and the degree to which the movement of capital reinforces the power of the consumer are fundamental to how free markets operate. A well-functioning market allocates resources, including capital, to create the greatest possible consumer satisfaction as efficiently as possible. The discontented buyer will not remain a customer unless there is nowhere else to go, or it is too expensive to go elsewhere. In a competitive marketplace that offers meaningful consumer choice, firms that do well by their customers are rewarded by repeat business, lower price elasticity, higher reservation prices, more cross-selling opportunities, greater marketing efficiency, and a host of other things that usually lead to earnings growth. Economic growth is about producing more and better goods and services and about buyers and sellers engaging in more economic transactions. It is not too hard to find someone with something to sell, but how does one encourage consumers to engage in additional transactions? One way is to increase their satisfaction with the outcome of the transactions.

ECONOMIC GROWTH

The causes of economic growth have long been debated in economics. So too have the consequences. If improved consumer utility, as asserted by standard economic textbooks, is a standard for economic growth, it follows that consumers should be better off as the economy grows. GDP is a measure of the quantity of economic activity, but it says little about quality. Nevertheless, quality and quantity generally go together.[11] This is evident in the relationship between customer satisfaction and GDP. As Benjamin Friedman finds, economic growth is consistent with both producing more and producing better. Consumer satisfaction and household spending are at the center of the free market. In one way or another, everything else—employment, prices, profits, interest rates, production, and economic growth itself—revolves around consumption. Without it, there would be no incentive to produce (and obviously no employment). Consumer spending alone makes up more than two-thirds of GDP in the United States—more than $11 trillion per year. In China, it's closer to one-third, but the proportion is growing. If consumers reduce their spending by as little as 1 to 2 percent, the economy slows. If they increase spending, albeit by a little more than a percentage point or two, the effect is the opposite. No other category or group of decision makers—not the government, not business—has comparable economic powers.

The stagnating rate of progress has led to a slowing rate of improvement in living standards, of course. This has been evident in most developed nations since the 1970s. Except for a brief period in the late 1990s, GDP growth in the United States has been tepid since 1973. But in the broader sense, *world* economic growth is now the highest we have seen in 30 years. Not only have consumers benefited from an increasingly global supply of goods and services, much of it readily available on the Internet, but hundreds of millions of people have joined the global labor force. Because of the advances in communications technology, workers don't have to move to where the jobs are; the jobs are moving to where the workers are.

Putting together the forces of global capitalism, the growing power of the buyer, the rising cost of time, and the transformation of advanced economies from manufacturing to service, it's important that we grasp the implications. They are central to how we view productivity and the leverage of company assets, and to how we manage customer relationships. It is also important to recognize that there are exceptions to this picture because there are forces that move in the reverse direction. For example, in the area of energy, where supply is scarce; it's not a buyer's market, and the product is not intangible. Here, we have a very different set of circumstances, more akin to the days when supply ruled and demand followed. But for the most part, we will have to adapt to an economy of intangibles, for which the economic assets are different, measurement is different, and the notion of scarcity is different. The nature of competition, when buyers are powerful, is also different. Growth hinges on how production and its input, including labor, best fit together and the ease with which buyers and sellers can find one another. The process is driven by the buyer. In accounting, whether national or corporate, growth is recorded when there is an economic transaction and money changes hands. We have already talked about GDP. Let's now understand how it is put together. If we add the value of all economic transactions plus investment and adjustments for export-import (where the end user is involved in order to avoid double counting) over a year, we get the gross domestic product (GDP). So the issue of economic growth, for companies and for nations, is one of encouraging buyer-seller transactions.

Let's look at the most basic level of any economic exchange. It occurs because a seller has something to sell that a buyer is able and willing to pay for. The seller's motivation is to make a profit. The buyer's motivation is satisfaction. In a service economy, transactions aren't discrete. Most of them are ongoing, usually until the buyer doesn't have a need for the service anymore, finds a better alternative, and/or becomes dissatisfied. In this sense, most economic transactions are repeat exchanges. Most revenue and profit come from repeat business in most companies. It's in everybody's interest that buyer-seller transactions are repeated over time and that they are ongoing. What might the factors be that would encourage this? What would create repeat transactions? The answer is as simple as it is obvious. If both parties—buyers and sellers—got what they wanted out of the deal, both would want to repeat the experience. In an economy where the buyer becomes increasingly powerful vis-à-vis the seller, it is the satisfaction of the buyer that holds the key to repeat business for the seller. Increasing customer satisfaction encourages more consumer demand, which of course leads to more consumer spending, which, in turn, has a big effect on GDP growth.

At the macro level, ACSI data have shed more light on causes and consequences of economic growth. If improved consumer utility (i.e., satisfaction) is indeed a standard for economic growth, it follows that consumers should be better off as the economy grows, and vice versa. Changes in aggregate satisfaction are related to GDP growth both as precursors, via their impact on household spending, and as a contemporaneous reflection of higher consumer utility. A positive outcome from a buyer-seller transaction makes both parties inclined to repeat the experience (more production, more consumption). A negative outcome is likely to have the opposite effect. Thus, consumer satisfaction is not only a beneficiary of economic growth but a contributor to it as well.

The relationship between aggregate customer satisfaction and GDP growth is pretty strong and it does suggest that the satisfaction of the customer is an important element not only for the individual business firm, but also for the economy as a whole. It is hardly a stretch to suggest that the way consumers spend money must have something to do with their anticipated satisfaction. Yet, this has more or less escaped the forecasters of consumer spending. Perhaps the shifting balance of power between buyers and sellers and the growth of supply have made conventional theories of consumption obsolete.

Milton Friedman was awarded the Nobel prize in economics in 1976. Franco Modigliani got it in 1985. In both cases, their contribution to understanding consumer spending played a major part. Friedman's theory says that household wealth determines spending: A change in household wealth, which he calls permanent income, will cause a change in spending. Modigliani expanded on the idea, suggesting that spending must equal the annuity value of lifetime resources and that these resources are different across people's life cycles. But these theories have not predicted consumer spending. Many economists assume that markets are efficient, and if true, wealth cannot be predicted. Thus, the reasoning goes, spending cannot be predicted, either—if the cause of spending is unpredictable, spending itself must also be unpredictable. But a good deal of human behavior can be reasonably well predicted—either from observation or (better) by understanding the forces that motivate behavior.

In addition to Friedman and Modigliani, there is John Maynard Keynes, of course. The Keynesian consumption theory attributes changes in income as the cause of changes in spending. This theory has not been very successful in predicting consumer spending either. Income is not a motivator—it is a means.

George Katona, originally from Budapest, Hungary, and generally considered the founder of economic psychology, had a different idea. He is much less a familiar figure than Milton Friedman or John Maynard Keynes, but our data suggests that he was on the right track. Katona received a doctorate in experimental psychology in Germany in the early 1920s and was on the faculty at the University of Michigan from 1946 until his death in 1981. After graduation, he took a job as an economic journalist. When in 1933 Hitler confiscated the publication for which he worked, Katona left for the United States. Germany not only faced the ascent of the Nazis but was also plagued by hyperinflation, for which there was no good economic explanation. Katona was convinced that inflation could not be explained by economics alone, but that it had a psychological dimension as well. His ideas about consumer spending were very different from those of Keynes and Friedman. In essence, he suggested, that changes in spending had to do with two major factors: the consumer's ability to buy and the consumer's willingness to buy. Ability to buy is, of course, related to both Keynes and Friedman. But it should not be, according to Katona, the central focus. Rather, it acts more like a constraint. The key is the "willingness to buy." If a consumer is "willing" to buy, financial constraints might prevent it. But somebody would not purchase simply because he or she was able to. To predict consumer spending, Katona developed the Consumer Sentiment Index (CSI), which showed some impressive results early on. Since then, the ability of the CSI to predict consumer spending has been more modest.

But Katona's work was done some 50 years ago and the economy is different today. The consumer is different as well—especially the American consumer. The modern U.S. consumer has no apparent fear of tomorrow and doesn't feel the same financial constraints as the consumer of the 1950s. If income is wanting, credit is (almost) always available. In 2005 and 2006, Americans spent everything they earned and then some, pushing the personal savings rate down to a level not seen since the Great Depression.[12] While a low savings rate is nothing new in the United States, it hasn't been negative since 1933. But it is easy to understand why it was negative in those days. Twenty-five percent of the labor force was without jobs and people dipped into their savings in order to buy food and clothing. Today, there's no such excuse. Only the extent to which the debt burden becomes a problem does spending seem to be curtailed. Our research findings indicate that there are two essential factors at play: the willingness to buy (which of course is closely related to the satisfaction the consumer expects) and the size of debt relative to income. The latter has an effect only if debt is high. Accordingly, consumer spending in the United States today has a great deal to do with customer satisfaction. It has more impact than any other factor we have tested. There is also a scientific explanation for this, but it doesn't come from economics or psychology. Instead, it comes from magnetic resonance imaging and neuroscience.

There are separate parts of the brain that react when we are faced with gains versus losses. In the context of consumer purchase behavior, it means that consumers are trading off the immediate satisfaction of acquiring something against the immediate pain of parting with money. However, the pain can be postponed by the use of credit. People are conditioned to seek gratification in just about everything they do. Consumer behavior is no exception. If the pain of paying can be postponed, what's left is instant gratification. That's why customer satisfaction predicts spending. It also explains why the use of credit has grown to such a level that savings are close to negative.

Things are different in other countries. In Japan, the problem is the reverse. Consumers save too much and spend too little. This is the case in China as well. Curiously enough, the inclination for saving in these countries makes U.S. consumer spending easier to predict. The savings in Japan and China compensate for the lack of savings in the United States. They finance the spending habits of American consumers.

It didn't use to be this way. Americans, like other nationals, were not exempt from the law of the pocketbook and used to forego a portion of today's consumption in order to be better off tomorrow. As long as everybody didn't forego too much at the same time, this was a recipe for economic growth, with more goods and services produced and consumed. But in a global economy, it's not surprising that the financing of one country's consumption comes from other counties. As long as Asian investors see the benefit in supporting American consumers, this will continue. And the spending habits of American consumers become more predictable since income, household wealth, and other financial restrictions matter less. As a result, what matters most to the consumer not overly burdened by immediate financial lia-bilities is the gratification or satisfaction derived from consuming products and services.

Most human behavior involves a search for gratification, and eco-nomic behavior is no exception. Obviously, the satisfaction people obtain from shopping, buying, and consuming has something to do with their future discretionary spending. Spending is not determined by ability to pay (income, household wealth, etc.), but by anticipated satisfaction. Because consumer expenditure reflects the valuation of the satisfaction from the products and services bought, there is an obvious relation between spending and satisfaction.

Changes in customer satisfaction don't merely shift consumer preference from one company to another, but they also affect industry demand and the general willingness of households to buy. The impor-tance of this can hardly be overstated. Since its inception, the data show that the ACSI has accounted for more of the variation in future spending growth than any other factor, be it economic (income, wealth) or psychological (consumer confidence).

Is it risky for Americans to allow so much of their economic fate to be in the hands of non-American investors? It may sound strange that the richest country in the world borrows money from developing countries. It gets good terms to boot. Shouldn't it be the other way around? If you think about it, it's actually not that different from the saving and consumption patterns of individual households. Wealthy households borrow a great deal more than poor ones and they often get better terms from the lender. In the global economy, it is possible for a country's population to consume more than it produces. It is also possible to export less than what's imported and spend more than earned. As long as other countries are filling the gap by saving more and putting some of their investments into the United States, what we have is a consequence of trade and economic incentives. The financing of U.S. consumption, primarily by China and Japan, is a way for these countries to promote their exports, increase employ-ment, facilitate economic growth, and build up capital reserves to cushion sudden disruptions in capital markets.[13] From a global economic perspective, there are forces that offset the risk as well. A severely devalued dollar and a shrinking U.S. economy wouldn't be in the interest of Japan and China, because that would reduce the value of their dollar holdings and reduce U.S. demand for their products.

Aside from the fact that the satisfaction of the customer takes on an even more prominent role in predicting consumer spending, customer satisfaction is related to trade imbalances in another way. But we rarely think of customer satisfaction in this context. It's much more common to deal with trade deficits in the context of currency devaluation, or legislation. For example, as far as the United States is concerned, a weaker dollar might help, but it also would bring higher interest rates. Legislation designed to protect companies from foreign competition might help as well, but it would have adverse effects for global economic growth. For countries with high trade deficits, one might be better off designing policy for stimulating upward shifts in demand for domestic products. That's what higher customer satisfaction does. Improved quality, if recognized and appreciated by the consumer, leads to higher satisfaction and causes an upward movement in demand curves. Higher interest rates and protectionism have the opposite effect. They are not beneficial to customer satisfaction and don't cause an upward shift in demand.

What would be beneficial is to move accounting into the twenty-first century. If investments in customer service were capitalized over time, we would have a much better grasp on how firms make money and we would see a reversal of the weakening relationship between a company's assets and its future performance. It would also be much more consistent with how the overall economy works and with the new theories of economic growth.

But obviously, satisfaction is not discernible in the sense that we can see or touch it. Contrary to price, sales, or units of production, satisfaction is not "publicly observable." This may be a problem to accountants, but the unobservable nature of a subject matter has not prevented psychologists from trying to measure intelligence, motivation, personality, etc., nor has it stopped polling firms from attempting to quantify public opinion. But it was not until fairly recently that a new set of much more rigorous and powerful methods for measurement became available for analyzing that which cannot be observed.

Not only can one now objectively assign numbers to such variables, it is also possible to incorporate the unobservable into causal systems of latent variable equations. While personal experience and satisfaction are subjective, their measures are not. Among the sciences, modern physics has led the way here, as it has been confronted by statistical relationships, black holes, system behavior, and theory-laden observations. While black holes may be a bit challenging for the dismal science, many economic phenomena are also truly unobservable. Even though "experience" and "satisfaction" are private matters, it doesn't mean that they are inaccessible to measurement or too illusive for scientific inquiry. The ACSI falls in the category of unobservable experience-based utility; it is not derived from observable choice but designed to predict it.

In economics, where the nature and the growing importance of intangible assets seem to be gaining more attention, some very basic assumptions are now being cast aside. Just take the notion of being able to have the cake and eat it, too. The increasing prevalence of nonrival goods will create a potential for much stronger economic growth than we have seen in the past. The law of diminishing returns doesn't apply here. Take knowledge, for example. You can give it (or sell it) to somebody else, but that doesn't mean that you don't have it anymore. To the extent that knowledge can be packaged into software or other scalable products, there are increasing rates of returns. The allocation of scarce resources has been a key principle in economics, but it's now been joined by another perhaps even more forceful and more exciting possibility—the economics of abundance.

But the revolution in the halls of academe has not been noticed much in the national debate, in the press, or in business. Paul Romer is not exactly a household name (in fact, his father Roy, the former governor of Colorado, is probably better known), but his work has had a huge impact on how we look at the sources for economic growth. Romer was the first economist to explain how falling costs were attributable to a growth in knowledge. Since the rate of progress has been slower in the past 50 years compared with the 50 years preceding it, economic growth was slower as well. Romer doesn't say this, but that's my interpretation. But now, we have an explosion in the production of nonrival goods. We're already seeing the consequences in strong world economic growth. Nonrival goods are available to all consumers without mutual interference. There's no inherent mechanism of exclusion. This is well described in David Warsh's excellent book.[14] If I eat a hamburger, the same burger cannot be eaten by you, because the hamburger is a rival good. A nonrival good is something that isn't used up after it has been consumed. When I watch a movie, I have not prevented another person from watching it. The same is true for books, software, and recipes. The utility I get doesn't infringe on the utility of others using the same product. Then there are products for which my utility is greater because you are using them, too. What good would the telephone be, if I was the only one who had one? These are the kind of products that have come to the forefront in the modern economy, the most obvious of which are those based on the Internet. They will be the source of the new economic growth—the most powerful since the industrial revolution. Though allocation of scarce resources will still be important, economic growth will be fueled by unbounded abundance—both in terms of the products themselves, but also in terms of information as a facilitator for organizing production and communicating to, from, and between buyers.

The phenomenon of increasing rates of return is not isolated to nonrival goods. We can also get it from leveraging intangible assets. Consider the return on customer assets? Let's do some simple algebra. Suppose that 40 percent of our customers return each year and purchase the same product at the same price. Each year, we lose 60 percent of the customer asset value and our average customer buys 1.6 products from us ($1/.6 = 1.6$). I am simplifying a bit here, but just enough to make the point simple without sacrificing too much reality.

What happens if we manage to keep 50 percent of your customers? Now, we get 2 purchases on average (1/.5 = 2). What if we do exceptionally well in terms of customer retention? Suppose we get 80 percent. That would be 5 purchases (1/.2 = 5). At 95 percent, we get 20 purchases. Increasing rates of returns to the extreme. We have gone from 1.6 purchases at a customer retention of 40 percent, to 2 purchases at a retention rate of 50 percent, 5 at 80 percent, and 20 at 95 percent. That's an asset value growth of 25 percent, 150 percent, and 300 percent!

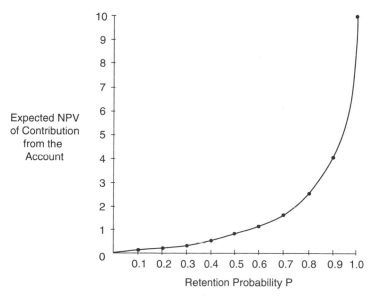

Figure 2.1   Retention Economics

The new growth theory in economics, revolutionary as it may be, is still about supply and how to best arrange factors of production. But growth also requires a buyer. Production alone doesn't count. And here is another major factor: New technology makes it easier for buyers and sellers to find one another. To the extent that business transactions are facilitated via new technology, growth will benefit. To the extent that both parties go into the deal with more information and better knowledge, the probability of a good outcome improves as well: Satisfaction for the buyer, profit for the seller. The demand curve moves upward. Overall consumption utility goes up. Everybody gains. The economy grows. Business grows. Consumers become more satisfied. Now, combine the expansion of nonrival goods with the developments in information technology—the web in particular—(which itself is fundamentally nonrival) and we have a platform for explosive economic growth. But we also have to harness its power. And, again, most of this power belongs to the buyer—not the seller, the manufacturer, or the service provider.

STOCK PRICES

How can one tell if a company is doing well or what its prospects for the future might be? Although this is what business schools teach and management consultants sell, the answers to these questions have remained elusive. The economy—for nations and for companies—has changed, while its measurements have not. The shift in economic activity from manufacturing and mass production toward service and information exchange has been massive. Yet, national and corporate accounting systems cling to asset measurement that lost its relevance decades ago. The Commerce Department still reports on pig-iron production. Corporate accounting is blind to assets that matter the most.

But not everything has changed. It is important to separate that which has changed from that which hasn't. Clearly, some things remain the same and are unlikely to change in the future. Fundamental economic behavior and basic economic objectives have *not* changed. Economic behavior is still about choice and allocation of resources. The maximization of asset value is still a fundamental objective and the value of the combined assets of a company is still equal to the expected net discounted value of its future cash flows. Companies still compete for customers' favoritism in order to maximize the value of these flows. Gaining customer favoritism for long-term value depends on customer satisfaction.

If financial prices reflect all relevant public information all the time, as suggested by efficient markets theory in finance, it would be a fluke if somebody consistently beat the stock market. Indeed, it is difficult to find somebody who has. Of course, it would be equally difficult for someone to do worse than the market. That is, even if one really tried to make the most stupid investments imaginable, it wouldn't be possible to consistently defy the laws of probability.

If, on the other hand, knowledge and experience make a difference, one would expect money managers and security analysts to have an edge in picking stocks. Regardless of whether markets are efficient or not, one would not expect professionals to consistently underperform the market.

So how can it be that they have? A good deal has been written about conflicts of interest due to the fact that most analysts work for investment bankers, but that doesn't explain why professional stock pickers, on the average, consistently bet on losers. If they generally look to buy low and sell high, but systematically fail to beat random stock picks, perhaps the information they use is systematically distorted. I have already alluded to such distortions and one doesn't have to look hard to discover them. The disconnect between the historical costs of assets, which is what is recorded on the balance sheet, and their market value keeps growing.

The value of any asset, tangible or not, is always determined by the expected benefits it will generate—just as the value of a company equals the sum of the expected net value of its cash flows. The cash flows related to business operations come from customer revenue and the cost of acquiring and serving customers. That's it. Period! Both are determined by the customer asset. As far as other assets are concerned, their value is determined by their net contribution to enhancing the customer relationships. If an asset, whether recorded on the balance sheet or not, contributes nil, directly or indirectly, to the customer asset, its value is also nil, no matter what the balance sheet says. For example, a company's employees are often a valuable asset, not recorded on the balance sheet. But employees are only valuable in the context of their contribution to customer acquisition and customer retention. Their contribution doesn't have to be direct, but there has to be some sort of positive contribution beyond the replacement cost of the worker.

THINKING IN TERMS OF ASSETS

Now then, let's go back to the challenge to my MBA students in advancing the discussion on economic value creation or how to make money. Any issue, question, or problem that one might want to resolve depends on context. When I first asked the question about how to make money, I didn't provide context and thus, didn't get constructive answers. Now, let's go back and tackle the same issue again, but within the context of prediction, rising buyer power, time inflation, good and bad productivity, and intangible assets.

Rather than thinking in terms of creating products for which there is a great market need or trying to figure out how one can buy cheap and sell dear, it's more useful to think in terms of economic assets. How do I get, develop, and control relevant assets? An economic asset produces future income for the owner of that asset. So if I own or control a good asset, that's what's going to happen. I will make money in the future. Asset pricing has little to do with the past. We may have assets that produced great returns in the past, but the past matters only if extended to the future. For example, Apple had record profits in the fourth quarter of 2006. Sales reached record levels as well. Analysts' expectations were exceeded by a wide margin. You'd think stock price would go up. Well, Apple's stock plunged. Stock prices don't have much to do with past profits or exceeding expectations. But they have everything to do with expectations about the future. In this case, the future prospects suggested by past performance were trumped by a disappointing forecast.

Tapping the sources of cash flows is what Customer Asset Management is about. Its objective is to increase the level and speed of net cash flows and to reduce the uncertainty (risk) associated with them. This is different from expressing business objectives in terms of sales, revenue, market share, or even bottom-line profitability, but it is consistent with creating shareholder value. Our research findings point to two key factors that lead to shareholder value: (1) the strength and magnitude of customer relationships and (2) capital efficiency. If financial reports included information on customer relationships, there would be a much better understanding of the link between the firm's current condition and its future capacity to generate shareholder wealth. Managers who improve customer satisfaction will create shareholder value. Investors who pay attention to the health of the firm's customer relationships will make better investment decisions. So what do we know about customer satisfaction? What is it? What's causing it? How can we measure it? Let's take a look at the science.

CHAPTER 3

The Science of Customer Satisfaction

A few years back, I was asked by the *Harvard Business Review* to write a short piece entitled "The Science of Satisfaction."[1] Actually, it didn't deal that much with science, but made the point that efforts to improve customer satisfaction were typically recorded as costs before the benefits of the efforts were realized. As a result, many companies overstated earnings in one period and understated them in another. Other companies—Compaq, Dole, Nike, AT&T, and Kmart among them—were having difficulty maintaining the satisfaction levels of their customers and saw stock prices suffer as a result. I am not going to dwell on the details of science here either, but it will be useful to talk about some fundamentals. No math required. No assumption of familiarity with scientific methods. What I would like to do is to use science for systematic analysis and for substantive knowledge. And, at a minimum, sound an alert about the boundaries of the most common "do-it-yourself" approaches guided by nothing but a desire for simplicity. Simplicity is all good and well, but it sometimes comes at a high price. Let's start with measurement theory.

If done without the benefit of science, assigning numbers to objects, which is what measurement is about, is meaningless at best, and misleading at worst. It would be like trying to build a bridge without knowledge of structural engineering. Fortunately, most bridges *are* constructed by engineers. The fact that they are often not well maintained is another matter. Regrettably, most measures of customer satisfaction are more like the rough-and-ready kind—patched together without the benefit of statistics, mathematics, or measurement theory. A sort of, "let's just ask our customers" mentality seems to dominate in many companies.

Management consulting firms have been of no help. In some ways, they have made the problem worse by ignoring measurement theory all together. There should be no mystery about what it has led to. Bridges constructed without knowledge of structural engineering will collapse; data obtained without a knowledge of how to assign numbers to objects create random noise with large margins of error, and lead to costly mistakes.

According to a survey done just after George W. Bush had denounced the International Criminal Court, most of his supporters were pleased that that he was in favor of it.[2] Or so they said. Survey respondents say many things, some true, some not, and some that make no sense. On the average, even a professionally conducted survey has about 30 percent error for each question, above and beyond sampling error. Even responses to the simplest questions are not error-free. The U.S. Census Bureau has a question about male vs. female. Respondents are instructed to check ONE box: male or female. Either, or. If applied to the total U.S. population, about 150,000 people check *both* boxes. This is either because gender is viewed as a continuous variable or because the respondents don't know, make a mistake, etc. Whatever the cause, the responses are difficult to interpret. I have seen many companies allow unfiltered survey responses affect strategy and bonus payments to employees. There is always random noise in raw data, but a good measurement system can convert noisy and imperfect raw data into accurate, forward-looking, relevant, and actionable information. Here's where mathematics and statistics, as well as measurement theory, enter the picture. We now have methods to sort out the relevant from the irrelevant, filter out noise and error, take us from description to explanation, from samples to populations, and from empirical relationships to an understanding of what causes what. Paradoxically enough, quantification has become standard practice in professional management, but the measurement itself is rarely subjected to professional standards and its accuracy is often questionable.

Scientific discipline brings discipline. It forces beliefs into the open, makes assumptions testable and lets us build on what's known. For example, we know that, under most circumstances, there is a positive relationship between product quality and customer satisfaction. We might not know how strong this relationship is, because it varies from company to company, but in all probability, it's not negative. While this may seem trivial, determining the strength of the relationship is anything but. There are also circumstances when the seemingly obvious is false. Take the relationship between price and customer satisfaction, for example. If price is reduced, conventional wisdom suggests that the value of the product (to the buyer) increases. As a consequence, the satisfaction of the customer should go up. This may well be the case, but a price reduction could also have the exact opposite effect. I am not talking about the kind of luxury good where price is a proxy for quality and the demand curve has a positive slope (i.e., the higher the price, the greater the demand), but something more troublesome and surprising to managers who face it. Aside from the effect that comes from inferring quality from price, why would a drop in price lead to lower customer satisfaction? Suppose that you have a favorite brand and that you, like most people, have certain budget constraints. Whether that brand is a car or a bar of soap, and almost regardless how satisfied you are with it, your loyalty is neither absolute nor immune to marketing efforts by other sellers. In fact, you may be tempted by another brand's discounted price. Suppose you switch, however temporarily, to the discounted brand—not because you like it better, but because of the discount. Are you going to be more satisfied? Your pocketbook may be thicker, but you're not likely to be more satisfied.

Neuroscience tells us that the opposite is likely to be true. In the aggregate then, what happens to the company that got buyers to defect from their favored brand? It will see a sales bump *and* a drop in customer satisfaction, followed by lost sales later on. It will get a bunch of new customers who'd rather be somewhere else. These customers will leave unless the price concessions continue or get bigger. Ford, DaimlerChrysler, and General Motors learned this the hard way by mortgaging their future business with short-term price fixes. And the U.S. automobile industry has seen the largest exodus of workers in any industry in any part of the world. I am not suggesting that rebates are entirely to blame for this, but when you are trying to sell cars that the buyers don't have enough affection for, you don't have much pricing power.

LEARNING THE WRONG LESSON THE HARD WAY

Tangible assets—as recorded on the balance sheet—account for a rapidly shrinking portion of company value. Intangible assets now represent about as much as 70 to 80 percent of the market value of the Dow Jones Industrials. The same is true in most developed countries.

The customer asset is one such intangible asset. In a competitive marketplace where buyers have choice and information about alternatives, the value of the customer asset is determined by how satisfied customers are, the likelihood of doing future business with them, interest rates, and the profit margin. Satisfied customers are not only the most consequential economic asset, but they are also a proxy for the sum total of the value of all other company assets—virtually all costs and revenues have some relationship, however weak or indirect, to customer acquisition and customer retention. If not, why spend the money? If (nonfinancial) revenue doesn't come from customers, where does it come from? Thinking about company assets in this way challenges the short-term strain that pervades most American and, to a lesser extent, European businesses. Because cost cutting has an immediate effect on profit, short-term pressures from capital markets encourage it. Conventional accounting practices don't help either. They too favor cost cutting.

Writing about what he called "The Performance Measurement Manifesto," Robert Eccles of the Harvard Business School reminds us that revolutions begin long before they are recognized.[3] It's now more than 20 years since executives began to rethink how to measure business performance. But so far, the impact has not been great. At its core, the idea is that financial numbers are limited to what they tell us about the future—and we already know the past. But there is a shift from financial numbers as the foundation for performance measures to other sets of measures that are mostly nonfinancial. Looking back, there was a lot of experimentation with a variety of tools in the 1980s and 1990s. We had Six Sigma, AQL (Acceptable Quality Level), CIP (Continuous Improvement Process), JIT (Just-in-Time), Poka-Yoke (making the Workplace Mistake-Proof), QFD (Quality Function Development), SPC (Statistical Process Control), SQC (Statistical Quality Control), TQC (Total Quality Control), TQM (Total Quality Management) and FFU (Fitness for Use). We saw balanced score cards, benchmarking, best practices, and even metrics on user eyeball movements on the web. Many of these vanished after the 2000 stock market bubble burst, when the very companies most eager to adopt nonfinancial measures got hammered the hardest. As a result, business reverted back to a greater reliance on "hard numbers." Nonfinancial measures are still with us, and slowly regaining some of their previous status. But the problem has been the failure to find a relationship between intangible assets and tangible profits. If that's the case, why leverage the intangible? An enormous amount of stock market value was lost in 2000, but no matter how painful the lesson, it wasn't learned well. The failure in finding the relationship to profits wasn't because the relationship doesn't exist—it was because the wrong metrics were used and the measurement technology was too primitive. For example, I doubt whether eyeball movements have much to do with economic returns or that raw data from customer surveys can say anything useful about customer assets.

The modern economy puts extraordinary importance on the value of information itself. There has been tremendous progress in the transmission of information. We have major industries whose business is to collect and sell information. Since information is a nonrival good, growth has been explosive. But the more valuable information has become, the lower its average quality. The demand for information has accelerated so much that it is outstripping the ability of its users to distinguish bad from good. This is a big problem and it is evident in many kinds of organizations in both the private and public sector. It's especially problematic in the quantification of qualitative data: A number is a number and once its inaccuracy is discovered, it may be too late. People have moved on. Memory is short. Whenever demand causes abundance of supply and unit prices fall, the average quality of supply seems to drop.

What do we need to know to do better? How can we recognize a measurement dud when we see one? Measurement theory can help. Its origin goes back to physical attributes, such as mass and length, which have the same intrinsic mathematical structure as positive real numbers. Modern management is a devotee of Lord Kelvin, who considered knowledge to be meager and unsatisfactory if it cannot be expressed in numbers. But "knowledge" is illusory if the way in which the numbers are assigned is incorrect or sloppy. As customers, we all have had an experience with surveys in which one question is dumber than the next. In one of its customer satisfaction surveys, KLM Royal Dutch Airlines asks its passengers: "To what extent do you agree with the following statement (strongly agree, agree, disagree, strongly disagree):

"Things like meals and movies should happen when I want them."

I am not making this up. I was asked to complete the survey myself. KLM thanked me for my efforts, and advised me that "your valued opinion will help improve our understanding of your needs regarding our services."

Didn't KLM already know that passengers want meals and movies when they want them and that they don't want them when they don't want them? What's a passenger to think? Can management be that incompetent? Would that go for the pilots too? Is this airline safe to fly? Or is it that the airline doesn't care about its passengers? Does any airline care? The airline business doesn't have high levels of passenger satisfaction. Most airlines have financial difficulties. So, what's the problem? Fuel costs are increasing, fixed costs are high, labor relations are problematic, security issues abound, and the airports are crowded. But, as Michael Baiada has pointed out to me, the fundamental problem is one of poor management and reluctance to change. As he was commenting on our ACSI release for the airlines, he suggested that 80 percent of the industry's financial problems can be traced to basic quality management. What other industry delivers 40 percent to 50 percent of its product late and always has cost overruns of 10 to 20 percent? Why do airlines burn more fuel than needed? Why do they strand passengers in the aircraft for hours, depart early (leaving passengers behind), and waste fuel by flying faster than necessary only to wait for an open gate upon arrival? Even though the problems are of a very basic nature, it would be useful for airlines to know more about the marginal utility of the passengers. How important is on-time arrival? What about leg room? Food? Information? All these things need to be put together such that resources can be applied better.

THE FALLACY OF PERCENTAGES

Most firms report (and advertise) customer satisfaction in percentage terms: "85 percent of our customers are satisfied," "our customer satisfaction score is 90 percent," and the like. This is mostly nonsense. Such assertions are the same as measuring intelligence by asking "Are you dumb or smart"? The answers will not correlate to scholastic performance or to anything else for that matter. What intelligence and satisfaction have in common is that they are both unobservable and they are both matters of degree. Sure, you can be satisfied or dissatisfied, smart or dumb, but there is an underlying continuous property in both cases. Once we express something as the percentage of people expressing "satisfaction" or "dissatisfaction," we are not capturing the continuum. Information is discarded for the sake of black-and-white minimalism. That's a costly mistake. First, it leads to imprecision. Why would anybody want imprecise information? In statistical terms, the resulting number (estimate) has a large margin of error. In other words, noise looms large. The reason (or perhaps it's an excuse) for expressing customer satisfaction as a binary "either-or-proposition" is that it is "simple." But that's not the case. It's not simple. It's simplistic. And it is costly.

The imprecision of the information—which shows up in inexplicable random movements over time and makes it impossible to compare across products, regions, outlets, etc.—is contradictory to the purpose of measurement. Measurement is about precision. Imprecision is easy enough to get in other ways. Random noise is the opposite of precision. Obviously, random noise cannot predict future customer behavior. It cannot be linked to operations, either. Both links are critical. If the customer satisfaction measure cannot be tied to future financial performance, its economic relevance is lost. If it can't be tied to operations, managers can't execute.

WHAT TO DO?

All measurement instruments, be they cameras, x-rays, or survey questionnaires, require sufficient resolution. If a binary instrument is insufficient, how many scale points should there be in a customer satisfaction questionnaire? Three? Five? Seven? Ten? The most common scales in public opinion polls have two (agree, disagree), five, and seven scale points. But such scales don't have enough resolution for customer satisfaction. Yet, aside from percentages, they are very commonly used by companies today. So what's wrong with them? The answer has to do with frequency distributions. If one took a random sample of people's opinion of, say, McDonald's, Toyota, or Earl Grey tea, chances are that the responses would be distributed in the shape of a bell curve. That is, the responses would probably be normally distributed, with most of them in the middle and fewer at the end points of the scale. It turns out that a lot of things are normally distributed. It makes statistical analysis a lot easier when that's the case. But, although people's opinions may be normally distributed in general, customers' satisfaction isn't. And that's exactly the way it should be in a well-functioning economy. But it's not well understood. As a result, inappropriate scales and incorrect statistics are being used. Let me explain. Consider the tail of a bell curve in which the numbers are low. Here's where the really unhappy customers are. Suppose we are talking about Coca-Cola. One would expect to find very few customers in this tail. If you don't like Coke, you won't be a Coke customer for long. Bear in mind that we are not measuring the public at large, but customers. We are not measuring people who are not customers and for those who don't like Coke, the cost of going elsewhere is low. There are many other soft drinks available. And if that's not enough, there are other beverages. The buyer-seller exchange is quick, efficient, and not burdened by high costs per unit. On the buyer side, there is no learning cost to speak of, no service is necessary, and there is little buyer risk in moving from one product to another.

On the opposite side of the frequency distribution is where the satisfied customers reside. This tail is fat. People who buy Coca-Cola like Coca-Cola. If they didn't, they wouldn't continue to buy it. Now then, what does this mean for instrument resolution and the number of scale points? Let's try a scale of five points, with very satisfied and very dissatisfied as the end points. What will we get? To be sure, we're not going to see many ones, twos, or threes. These customers have already left. For all practical purposes, the five-point scale becomes a two-point scale and we're back to the problem of having a binary scale that doesn't have enough resolution.

Would a million scale points be better than 100 scale points? Obviously, the million scale point has greater resolution. A billion scale points would be even better. More is preferable, but always tempered by the respondents' ability to discriminate between scale points and the usefulness (to management) of additional granularity. So where do we end up? The general principle of non-normal frequency distributions holds in any market where there is sufficient consumer choice and where it's possible to go from one product to another without too much trouble. It's only when dissatisfied customers have nowhere to go or find it too expensive to get there, that we will get closer to a normal distribution. Statisticians would like that, but the rest of us wouldn't. The economist would see a market that's not functioning well. Dissatisfied customers would be locked into something they would prefer to get out of.

The mobile phone business has an element of customer lock-in that doesn't contribute to high levels of customer satisfaction. Most companies "lock in" their customers via a two-year contract. If service on the phone is needed, the contract is often extended. These contracts are not easily broken. There are termination costs and the full fee is typically applied by most mobile phone companies regardless of when the contract is due to expire. No wonder then that cell phones are among the lowest-scoring categories in customer satisfaction. Since most markets are fairly competitive and some have an abundance of buyer-choice options, a more granular measurement instrument would be desirable. A five-point scale isn't enough. Even a seven-point scale is questionable. We have found that ten-point scales do well. The responses exhibit a reasonable dispersion and respondents are able to discriminate between scale points. That's not the situation in public opinion polls, where the questions often pertain to things that the respondents are not all that familiar with. The opposite is true, of course, when the topic is one's own consumption experience.

In sum, what this means is that well-functioning markets, where there is enough buyer choice, suggest a scale of about ten points. Since the respondent, by definition, has actual experience, it's also possible to use the same type of scale in markets where there is some degree of monopoly power or in other contexts in which the freedom to choose is curtailed (e.g., government services).

MORE DELUSIONS

It is sometimes said that customer satisfaction is not particularly important and should not be measured. What's really critical, they say, is to have customers recommend your product. Aside from the fallacy of assuming that such recommendations will occur regardless of how satisfied the customers are (very few dissatisfied customers recommend products they are unhappy with), this has led to foolish measurement practices. What's done is usually something like the following: First, calculate the percentage of respondents who say that they are very likely to recommend a given product (say those who score nine or ten). Next, take those that score very low, say three to one) and calculate their percentage of the total. Now, you have the percentage of people who are very likely to recommend your product and the percentage of people who are not. Then, take the difference between these two percentages. If that number is positive, you have more customers who are likely to recommend your product than customers who aren't.

What's wrong with this? At first glance, it might sound reasonable. The problem has to do with how numbers are assigned: A perfectly good scale is ruined to the point that it generates very little useful information. A competent measurement methodology looks to minimize error. But here, the opposite is done. Instead of getting precision, random noise is produced. From a single scale, we have not only converted something continuous to something binary, but we have done it three times (percent of customers likely to recommend, percent of customers not likely to do so, and the difference between them). Each time, we have created a new estimate. All estimates contain error. Going from a continuous scale to a binary one introduces even more error.

If that's not enough, taking the difference between two estimates with error leads to exponentially greater error. In the end, we have produced a large amount of random noise, but very little information. When it comes to looking at changes over time, we further compound the problem. For each time period comparison, there are now six estimates and the final calculation is the percentage difference of customers that are likely to recommend. I have seen published reports sold for several thousand dollars in which almost all the reported change is due to random noise. For managers, it's bad enough to chase numbers they can't affect, but to chase randomly moving targets can do a great deal of harm to individual and company performance. Yet, it is not uncommon to find approaches of this kind. General Electric and Microsoft have both used some variant of them. It's not that these companies don't have competent statisticians or market researchers, but the decisions are often made at an organizational level where even rudimentary knowledge of measurement properties is slim.

There is no good reason for applying lax statistical standards for measurements about customers, especially not when measurement standards about product quality are rigorous. Product quality is obviously important for the future prospects of any company. But it's for naught if it doesn't register with customers. It is not quality per se that brings about economic returns—it is the improved consumption experience of the buyer that leads to repeat business and more demand. It's simple: Unless quality improvements shift the demand curve upward and/or reduce costs, quality investments don't pay off. For better or worse, such are the rules of a market economy.[4]

WHEN PERCENTAGES MAKE SENSE

So what do we do if everybody is set on percentages? I have faced this situation many times. Top management insists on having customer satisfaction expressed as a percentage. Usually, there are two reasons behind this. One has to do with a desire for simplicity.

Another is a concern of making too much of a break from the past. There is an argument for historical consistency, but it's a weak one. It makes little sense to keep repeating mistakes. That would compound the mistake and make future adjustments even more difficult. But change doesn't have to be abrupt. One solution could be to move from levels to changes. Both levels and changes in customer satisfaction contain important information although levels are more difficult to interpret. Like most economic data, be it profits at the micro level or GDP at the macro level, changes are often more meaningful. Changes can be expressed in percentages, without making incorrect assumptions or forcing a continuous measure into a binary one. The same logic can be applied when one wants to compare how satisfied customers are across different regions or different countries. Evaluating changes rather than levels is less complicated and less affected by individual, group, or cultural biases that play havoc with comparisons of levels.

Obviously, a measure of change implies a time horizon. The information cannot be gathered without the passage of time. Sometimes, there is little or no time available for making such comparisons. For example, it would be very useful to get information about the status of a company's customer relationships in mergers and acquisitions. In these situations, time is often of the essence and it might not be possible to get dynamic measures. If that's the case, we are stuck with levels. That doesn't mean levels of customer satisfaction need to be interpreted in a vacuum, however. A good benchmark may be the customer satisfaction levels of competitors. This too can be expressed in percentages. Take Dell, for example. In 2006, its ACSI score increased from its all-time low of 74 to a score of 78. That's not a bad score and it is a nice improvement, but it's not where Apple is. Not that these companies are competing head to head, but Apple was 6 percent above Dell in customer satisfaction. That may not sound like much, but it is. Since Apple moved into the number one ACSI position among PC makers in 2004, its stock price has gone up by about 800 percent. This is not all due to higher customer satisfaction—just like the low stock returns of Microsoft and

General Electric cannot be totally attributed to lack of customer satisfaction improvement—but it couldn't be done without it either.

FILTERING

Keep in mind why we measure. Measurement is about capturing information. Strangely enough, not all managers seem to recognize this. It strikes me as odd that IT departments in general seem not to have a great deal of measurement competence. After all, they deal with information. But they seem to be more concerned with transmission and compilation of data, without enough attention to what the data mean, how they are measured, and what purpose they serve. Many of the best IT companies have the worst performance measurement systems—especially when it comes to customer satisfaction. And yet, I think it was Bill Gates who proclaimed that whether you win or lose is determined by how you gather, manage, and use information. Gates is probably correct and his argument more compelling if posed in the negative. Bad measurement leads to bad information. Bad information leads to bad decisions. Bad decisions lead to competitive vulnerability. Competitive vulnerability leads to shrinking earnings and loss of capital. Show me a loser and I will show you a company with poor customer measurement systems. The reverse is not necessarily true, however. Microsoft's customer satisfaction is not high, according to ACSI, but because of Microsoft's size and power in the marketplace, it doesn't have to be. It's not that Microsoft's customer satisfaction is on par with monopolies, but it is lower than the average score for the industry.

The next phase in the information revolution will be purification, sorting and filtering. We have technologies for transmitting enormous amounts of data, but we don't yet have good systems for separating the bad from the good or the trivial from the relevant. The companies that excel here will have a much better chance at success than those that continue to use data in lieu of information. Data are the raw material from which information is made. Data must go through a cleansing process, a refinery, a filtering mechanism, and some form of analysis in order to be useful. Same with crude oil and gasoline. Cars don't run on crude oil. Companies should not run on raw data.

Once data has been converted to information, we judge its quality by: (1) accuracy, (2) relevance, and (3) actionability. Accuracy refers to precision, the ability to separate signal from noise and how representative the information is (how to generalize from the particular to the general). Relevance has to do with the impact on things that matter. Actionability calls for prescriptive information. That is, it should direct action. There are measurement systems about customer assets that satisfy these criteria. They are based on scientific principles, some of which involve fairly difficult mathematics and statistics. But conceptually, the principles are not difficult to grasp. I will try to explain them in prose rather than in equations. Let's start with the very notion of satisfaction itself. What is it and what do we know about it?

Economists have long expressed reservations about whether an individual's satisfaction or utility can be measured, compared, or aggregated. Classical economics, starting with Jeremy Bentham in the late eighteenth century, viewed consumer satisfaction and utility as equivalent. That is, utility was referred to as that property in any object, whereby it tends to produce benefit, advantage, pleasure, good, or happiness or to prevent the happening of mischief, pain, evil or unhappiness.[5] In neoclassical economics, the perspective is narrower. Utility is derived from observing how consumers choose.

Like economists would argue that stock markets can be efficient even though their participants can be irrational, George Katona thought that the summation of ignorance can produce knowledge because of self-canceling of random factors. The idea that the summation of ignorance can produce knowledge is pretty appealing. It's like finding nuggets of value in refuse. It is also consistent with the idea of filtering out noise in order to find a real signal, weak though it may be.

This brings us to the quantification of the unobservable. It may sound impossible that we can measure things we can't see and, perhaps even more astounding, that we can incorporate these unobservables into systems of equations that delineate causes and effects. The usual way to determine cause and effect is to go into the laboratory for systematic experimentation.

Starting with Sewall Wright's work with livestock, there are techniques that provide evidence of specific causal effects without laboratory experimentation. This is of great importance. Virtually all business decisions assume cause and effect. We lower prices to increase demand. We improve quality to increase customer satisfaction. It doesn't really matter whether we're on the road, trying to figure out how to get from point "a" to point "b," or whether we're trying to achieve some business objective. Same thing. We need to know where we are and where to go. It would also be helpful to know what happens once we get there. Business managers need to know the current status of customer relationships, how satisfied or dissatisfied customers are, what the value of the customer asset is, how to improve that value, and what the net effect is likely to be.

NEUROSCIENCE

Before we can quantify satisfaction, it might be useful to find out more about what it is. Recent findings by leading researchers in neuroscience have been illuminating. For example, Brian Knutson of Stanford finds that people get more satisfaction from anticipation of a purchase than from owning the item. David Blanchflower of Dartmouth quantifies the effects of satisfaction, income, and having sex. He estimates that a single person, not having much sex, needs to earn a minimum of $100,000 per year to be as satisfied as a married person.

What these scientists look at is the neurotransmitter, dopamine. This chemical transmitter is central to satisfaction. According to Gregory Berns, professor of psychiatry and behavioral sciences at

Emory University,[6] dopamine is released prior to consummation. It's a "chemical of expectation" with the purpose of committing our motor systems to a certain action. What this means is that satisfaction is the result of attainment of a goal and what one must do to get there. This is contradictory to the economic assumption that utility increases as the ratio of consumer input to output declines. Consumer input is usually thought of as money and effort. Output is the benefit the product generates.

Both neuroscientists and economists have long recognized that there is a difference between value and utility: People don't make decisions based on expected value but rather on expected utility—the satisfaction they hope to get or the punishment they hope to avoid.

Take the shark attacks in Florida, Virginia, and North Carolina in the summer of 2001. The disutility of getting eaten by a shark is high for most people. But the expected value of getting attacked by a shark is low (but like everything else, it varies with context). Beachgoers were getting alarmed by a growing incidence of shark attacks. Some suggested that this was simply because there were more people in the water. Others blamed President Clinton for having imposed shark-fishing limits. An editorial in *New York Times* (September 9, 2001) attempted to allay fears by pointing out that four times as many people were killed by falling television sets as were killed by white shark attacks in the twentieth century.[7] It was also suggested that the probability of getting killed in an automobile accident is much higher than being eaten by a shark.

I am not sure how useful it is to make these kinds of comparisons. In a way, they are nonsensical, because the context of the comparison is left out. If I go for a swim in the waters off the Florida coast, let's say at dusk when sharks tend to feed, the probability of getting attacked by a shark is more than a billion times greater than being killed by a falling television set or by a car (unless I was swimming under a bridge or very close to shore). On the other hand, when driving to work in Ann Arbor, the probability of a shark attack is next to zero (there are no definite predictions, if you believe in quantum mechanics).

Context and perspective always matter. Both relativity theory and quantum mechanics agree: Things don't exist in a vacuum. Where they don't agree is in the latter's assertion that we cannot make definitive predictions—not even in physics. Everything is probabilistic. And perspective matters here, too. From an individual's perspective, the probability of winning the lottery is extremely low. But the probability that someone will win is extremely high. One's satisfaction also depends on perspective and context. It's obviously subjective and differs from consumer to consumer. And it cannot be directly observed. The implication is that its measurement should vary according to context.

As Berns explains, if you like bananas better than oranges, then bananas have a higher utility to you than oranges. But only in a particular context. It doesn't mean that bananas give you more pleasure than oranges. There could be any number of reasons why, in any given situation, you pick bananas over oranges.

Whatever we do, and here too neuroscience corresponds to economics, we do with the expectation of a reward or avoiding being punished. The reward is satisfaction. Human behavior can be looked upon as a search for gratification. The brain region that integrates the planning of actions with potential rewards is found in the striatum. Because the striatum is where dopamine converges with information from the cortex, the striatum is where the brain motivations maps into actions. Here's where dopamine converges with information from the cortex. Dopamine is a chemical reward for the brain; and the striatum controls the conditions under which the dopamine is released. In other words, it holds the key to satisfaction. What was not known until recently is that dopamine is often released in advance of the reward. In other words, it operates as an incentive or motivator. The reward takes on a more expansive definition that includes not only the consumption activity, but the process of anticipating it as well.

PREDICTABILITY

The striatum responds more to unpredictable rewards than to predictable ones, but it is also true that predictability is essential for well-being. As I discussed in chapter 2, if I can predict some aspect of the future that others can't I have a competitive advantage. Predictability is about survival. Predicting better than others is about doing better—in whatever context you may want to apply it to. Wayne Gretzky was the greatest of hockey players because he knew where the puck was going before it got there. Roger Federer may be the best tennis player ever because he seems to know where his opponent is going to hit his next shot—perhaps even before the opponent himself knows. In a way, science works the same way, but we don't need God-given talent to benefit from it.

We use several so-called imputation techniques at CFI. What they allow us to do is to figure out what the answer to a question, posed to an individual, would be without asking the question and without getting a response. Even better, the answer is often more accurate than the response would have been. In simple terms, this is how it works: Suppose we have six questions for customer Joe. We ask him five of these and record his responses. For other respondents in our sample, we do the same thing, but we vary the omitted questions according to standard experimental designs. Now, given the fact that we have the answers to five questions from Joe, we can use the data from the rest of the sample to "impute" what Joe's answer to the sixth question would have been—and our imputation would be free from the usual survey problems of interviewer bias, misunderstandings, Joe's possible unwillingness to provide accurate responses, etc. We are using not only the pattern of responses from other responses, but a combination of information from Joe's answers to the five questions with the pattern of relationships between the responses for our total sample. To be specific, we predict what Joe would have answered. Not only do we reduce the cost of surveys in this manner, we also improve the quality of the data.

Steve Jobs seems to have an almost supernatural ability to predict the future better than his competition. Like Gretzky and Federer, he isn't right all of the time, but often enough. What Gretzky, Federer, and Jobs have in common is that they generalize from the unobservable better than the rest of us. Gretzky read patterns of the game better than anybody else. Federer's brain registers and computes the movement, balance, and tactics of his opponent in a fraction of a second. Jobs is able to combine a tweaking of already known technology with latent consumer demand in some of the most innovate ways any CEO has been able to do. For those of us with lesser talents for figuring out what the future will bring, whether we are talking about what is about to happen in a fraction of a second or years from now, there is science to guide us. Customer satisfaction cannot be observed, so we use indicators to measure it. Causes and consequences of satisfaction are known, but only partially. We can estimate the impact of causes not only on customer satisfaction, but on the resulting financial consequences as well.

Obviously, the future cannot be controlled by science anymore than Federer can control the level of play of his opponent. Even though there are general biological rules for the release of dopamine and the production of satisfaction, and even though we may have accurately determined the factors with the greatest impact on the satisfaction of our customers and subsequently improved our performance based on these factors, it is still possible that we might not get an improvement in customer satisfaction. Context can always trip us up. The context is so different from the waters off Florida to my car in Ann Arbor that it makes no sense to compare probabilities. The same principle is at play when competition is not sitting still, but moving fast, changing standards and perhaps even the rules of the game. But it is well to remember that the future is an extension of the past, albeit with a degree of unknown randomness, affected by forces of power in a systematic manner. The random part is usually small. If we know the past and the forces that fuel the systematic part, the future is ours to see.

DOING THINGS RIGHT, BUT LOSING ANYWAY

A few years back, we were working with a leading mobile phone company. It was clear that there were four "Key Action Areas" in which to improve customer satisfaction in the coming year. Two were product related and the others service related. The dilemma was that each of the Key Action Areas required a significant investment and might take more than a year to implement. Taking on all four would be expensive. But there was no choice. It was decided to improve across all of the key areas, but the allocation of resources was to be proportional to the impact on overall customer satisfaction. In this way, initiatives in the small business segment were balanced with the priorities of the residential and large business customer segments.

Despite these efforts, customer satisfaction dropped. Management was upset. Money had been spent, resources had been allocated, and careers were on the line. What had happened? Think back to context—a moving one.

As we poured over the data, a major culprit emerged: Internet services. It was one of the four Key Action Areas. The analysis showed that the company would be rewarded greatly for improvements in this area, but that it would be punished even more if it didn't improve. Sure enough, customers didn't see an improvement in the company's web service. We had great strides in the other Key Action Areas, but not enough to offset the lack of progress in Internet services. "But we have made progress and we are not standing still," objected one of the senior executives, citing a long list of things that the company had done to improve its web service. According to all objective standards, there had been considerable improvement. How is it possible that customer satisfaction can decline when most of its drivers have improved? Why were customers "experiencing" worse service now, when it was demonstratively better? And, worse, why was the effect overwhelming all the other positive things the company had done?

This is not as complicated as relativity theory in physics, but to some extent, it follows the same logic.

We didn't have to look far for the answer to the first question. The market demand for Internet services had tripled over the past year. The lower score was due to the fact that the company now had three times as many customers, many of whom had little experience with the company's product and services. Add that to the fact that it is always more difficult to serve more customers—not simply because it requires more resources, but also because more customers also bring added heterogeneity, which requires more service resources.

The second question requires a little more background, because it has to do with the fact that all measures are context dependent and everything is relative. Satisfaction is affected by changing circumstances and so is our measure of it. Before we field-tested various versions of the ACSI, I had reviewed all published research in the field and also looked at what companies around the world were doing. Although there was no consensus on how to measure customer satisfaction, three facets showed up over and over. The most common had to do with the confirmation or disconfirmation of prior expectations. Another was the idea of comparing a company's product to a customer's ideal version of the product—regardless of whether or not such a product even existed. The third facet was the cumulative level of satisfaction when all interactions, the customer's total experience over time with the company, were taken into account.[8] Accordingly, these three facets were translated into survey items and became indicators for the ACSI measure. By defining the unobserved satisfaction as a function of several observations, it was now possible to sort out the relevant from the irrelevant in the survey measures themselves (more about that in a minute). But this was not the only advantage. Another one was that the satisfaction variable would not be confounded with its causes. Most satisfaction indices simply lump a series of survey responses together, regardless of whether or not they are causally related. If they are, they should not be put in the same index, because it would then be impossible to take action since one cannot tell what's a cause and what's an effect. It wouldn't be possible to determine what the most important drivers of satisfaction are.

Having defined the satisfaction construct as a function of three variables, what does that function look like? There is no particular reason to make things more complicated than they are and a simple linear function will do in most situations. But what weight should the three indicators have? Can we just add the variables and take the average? Again, there is no reason to make things more complicated, but it would be too simplistic to simply take the average. The most useful weighting scheme is one in which the variables are weighted such that the impact of the resulting index is maximized with respect to the objective at hand. Indicators of satisfaction can be put together in an infinite number of ways. But it should be purpose that determines the tool—not the other way around. For most companies, the objective is to make money for its shareholders by serving customers well. In a customer satisfaction measurement system, that objective is translated into proxies (or leading indicators)—such as probability to repurchase, buy more, spread the good word, and so on.

But the reason for bringing up the mobile phone company here is that it is an example of what happens within the measurement system when the nature of competition changes and customers change as well; the weights of the indicators change too. This may cause concern about the ability to compare index values over time. If the weights are different from one time period to another, how can you compare? Well, what's the alternative? Set the weights in stone so that they cannot be changed? Technically, that would be simple and I know managers who are assured by the fact that things remain the same. But that assumes that the future remains the same, too. If it does, fine. Then it doesn't matter if the parameters are fixed to a constant; they will not change anyway.

Realistically, though, the satisfaction of our customers is not only dependent on what we do, but affected by what happens in the general environment as well. In our mobile phone case, the weight of the variable reflecting the distance to an ideal product had increased greatly. The company's score on that dimension had dropped. When customers compared the company's products to their ideal product, the company was not just coming up short; the importance of the comparison itself had taken on greater significance. It was now clear that the reason for the disappointing customer satisfaction results was that nobody was standing still. Competition was moving faster and doing things better. Customers changed. But things could have been worse. Management did improve product and service—however, it didn't improve relative to competition. But if it hadn't addressed the four Key Action Areas, it would have been left even further behind.

Meanwhile, in another part of the world, Xavier Quenaudon was scratching his head trying to figure out why one of the firms he was working with was getting *higher* customer satisfaction scores when it paid *less* attention to customer service. Xavier is a senior consultant and partner with CFI Group and has been with us from the early days. He, too, was working with a mobile phone company, but his company's situation was the opposite: Customer satisfaction improved even though its most important drivers did not. Xavier had found that improvements in the network were vital, so investments in the network's breadth (coverage) and depth (reliability) were intensified. Customer service was a secondary priority. He called Richard Gordon in the CFI office in Ann Arbor. Richard was analyzing the other side of the coin—the first mobile phone company I described—and the situation seemed contrary to logic until it was clear what was going on. In Richard's case, the company followed the research and did the right things, but had little to show for it because competition upped the ante. The improvements needed to be much greater.

Xavier told Richard about the company's background. It was launched in the mid-1990s and quickly became very successful, attracting customers looking for an inexpensive alternative to the more costly and expansive networks already in place. The business premise was that customers would be willing to accept a less-than-perfect network for lower rates, particularly if coverage in the largest cities was adequate.

Within two years of its launch the company had captured about 15 percent of the market, and after another two years, it was the industry leader in customer acquisition. Customer satisfaction climbed by 17 percent due to major network enhancements. But, a serious issue was rapidly emerging—one that could potentially lead to significant loss of customers if it wasn't dealt with quickly. Results from our measurement showed that, amid all the improvements, customers were becoming frustrated with service. While satisfaction improved, customer service plunged, and impact of the latter just about *tripled*.

What was going on?

Each year, the customer base doubled in size. As a matter of course, the company encouraged its customers to contact the company's customer service department for any question they might have. But the number of call center representatives remained largely the same, and the call centers became flooded with inquiries and problems that the service agents had difficulty handling. To make matters worse, the service policy was to answer calls (to reduce wait time) rather than to solve problems or respond to inquiries. But even so the average wait time rose well above what was deemed acceptable, and once a caller made it through to an agent, the query was often dealt with in a hasty and unsatisfactory manner. So why were customers more satisfied? Xavier and Richard discussed various possibilities and discovered that the problem with customer satisfaction was masked by high growth. This is one of the most dangerous situations that a company can be in. Growth without satisfied customers is not sustainable, but it may take some time for management to find out what's going on. Then, it will take time to fix the problem. In this case all customers were surveyed, but very few of the newly acquired customers found a reason to call service within the first six months. Customers were very pleased until they needed service assistance. That's when things broke down. And because the number of customers grew at such a rapid pace, the overall satisfaction looked very good, even as it was seriously weakened. This was a disaster in the making.

While management expected service performance scores to be poor, it was surprised by the impact analysis, which showed that customer service had become the area with the greatest effect on customer retention—and therefore a new priority of immediate concern. Consequently, investments were made, additional staff was hired, incoming call capacity enhanced, and a new IVR was implemented. But it took another year to see the payoffs. But much thanks to Xavier's work, disaster was avoided and the company was able to minimize the loss of customers and continue to grow at a healthy pace.

PRINCIPLES OF MEASUREMENT

A simple way to think about the relationship between (1) what we observe, (2) the unobservable, and (3) what is considered error comes from True Score Theory. This theory says that what we observe (O) equals some "true" (T) but unobserved "score," plus error (E). The equation is simple: "$O = T + E$," but one cannot solve it as it stands. There are two unknowns but only one equation. The known part is what we observe. The solution to most problems of this kind is to obtain more information and construct more equations. Suppose we have the notion (theory) that quality causes satisfaction, which, in turn causes loyalty. We cannot directly observe these variables. We can ask customers to rate quality, satisfaction, and loyalty, but then we are back to the problem of equating unobservables to responses to specific questions. It's not likely that these responses will unravel the actual unobservables to us. If they did, we would not have unobservables in the first place. Instead, let's go back to the military problem I discussed in the introduction. I knew we were looking for unmanned mini-submarines. We thought they were Russian. We assumed they were crawling at the bottom of the sea. That was about the extent of our theory. And then we had the pictures—the empirical "evidence." Each picture was the equivalent of a measuring stick. In a survey, each question is a "measuring stick." What we have to do is organize the measures according to our theory.

Suppose we measure "quality" from three questions that all deal with quality as experienced by the user; we have three questions that deal with how satisfied the respondent is; and we have three questions that aim to ascertain how likely it is that the respondent will come back in the future and buy again. The point I am making is that we need several measures of each concept that we are looking to quantify. It doesn't have to be three, it could be five, six, or ten, and in some cases even two, but we are now well on our way to solve the problem of too many unknowns with too few equations. For each measure, we now have an equation. For each of the three "quality" measures, we have the same unobservable. Our theory also implies that customer loyalty is a function of customer satisfaction (another equation) and that customer satisfaction is a function of quality (another equation). As it turns out, we have now enough data and enough equations to solve for the unobserved (using traditional statistical principles). We have also followed the principles of quantum mechanics by letting theory guide measurement. With a different theory (perspective) the solution to the unobservables would be different. But we don't need to appeal to quantum mechanics to make the point. As Peter Achinstein, a leading scholar in philosophy of science and a professor at Johns Hopkins University puts it, measurement without a theory is analogous to an interpreter without language.[9] Measurement is systematic and disciplined observation. Observation, if it is to have any meaning, must be interpreted. And, interpretation always involves theory in one way or another.

CAUSES AND THEIR EFFECTS

Not only can we now solve for the unobservable, but we can also provide evidence for cause and effect. Let's return to Sewall Wright. Perhaps he had difficulty seeing the beauty of poetry, but he did see casual relations where others saw correlations. Correlations don't imply anything about cause and effect. Anybody who has taken

Statistics 101 knows this. But Wright reasoned in the opposite direction. If we had a theory that could be expressed in terms of what the expected correlations were going to look like, *given* a theoretical specification of what's causing what, we could tell whether or not that theoretical specification was true or not. Let's go back to our (overly simplistic) theory to explain how this would work. Our theory says that quality leads to satisfaction and that satisfaction leads to loyalty. Most people would agree that this makes sense. But it is equally important to understand that what the theory doesn't say. In this case, our theory says that it is necessary for quality to be perceived by the buyer—otherwise, it won't have any effect on loyalty. But it doesn't say that quality improvements not recognized by consumers will have an effect on customer loyalty. It doesn't matter how much a company may improve quality if the customer does not appreciate the quality or is unwilling to pay for it. I have mentioned this before because it has serious implications, not only for how companies should gauge their investments in quality, but also for how we establish causes and effects in order to make better decisions. Our theory is explicit about an *indirect* link between quality and customer loyalty, via customer satisfaction. The links between the three variables are defined by what Wright called "path coefficients." In the more modern parlance of econometrics and psychometrics, they are called structural coefficients. If our theory is correct, we should be able to move from the path coefficients to correlations. The correlation between two variables is equal to the sum of all their connections, direct and indirect. Now then, the correlation between quality and customer loyalty is equal to the product of the links between quality and satisfaction and between satisfaction and loyalty, plus the link between quality and loyalty. But our theory says that the relationship between quality and loyalty can only work in an indirect manner—quality goes through customer experience (measured as satisfaction) in order to affect loyalty. In other words, our theory implies that the expected correlation between quality and loyalty is simply the product of the linkages between quality-satisfaction and satisfaction-loyalty. The direct link between quality and loyalty doesn't exist and is therefore equal to zero. So the test here is whether or not the theoretical model can get us back to the correlation coefficient. If the product of the quality-satisfaction and satisfaction-loyalty linkages equals the correlation coefficient between loyalty and quality, we have found evidence in favor of our theory's cause-and-effect hypothesis. Granted, this is a simple example, but it does show how the system works. In most applications, there are many more linkages, more measures, and more specifications about what affects what.

For most of the applications that we do at CFI, there is no analytical solution. But since computing power is not an issue today, as it is abundant and inexpensive, we are still able to find maxima or minima via search routines. I based many of the ACSI and CFI models on the Swedish statistician/econometrician Herman Wold's method of fix-point estimation. Under most circumstances, it is possible to have multiple solutions converge into one single solution by simply guessing what the end solution is for a given equation. Then, we estimate the solutions for other equations using our guesses as fixed parameters. In the next iteration, we go back to the first set of equations, throw away our guess work, and estimate a solution, based on fixing the most recent estimates from the other equations. We keep on iterating like this until we have a converging solution for which the numbers no longer change. The ACSI is a set of causal relations that link customer expectations, perceived quality, and perceived value to customer satisfaction. In turn, customer satisfaction is linked to consequences such as customer complaints and customer loyalty.

PRIMARY CAUSES OF CUSTOMER SATISFACTION

The most important driver for customer satisfaction has to do with "fit." The better the fit between buyers and sellers, the better the outcome. But "fit" is not what first comes to mind when managers think about how to improve customer satisfaction. It is more common to talk about quality or price. But fit is much more general and applies in just about every relationship—for spouses, dancing partners, bridge players, and singing duos. In a commercial setting, fit has to do with how well the seller's product matches what the buyer is looking for and what he is willing to pay. Fit is also not the responsibility of the seller alone. A well-educated and informed buyer who acts in a rational, responsible manner is more likely to emerge from economic transactions as a satisfied customer. A seller who is well-informed about what customers want and acts accordingly is more likely to create a satisfied customer. So what do customers want? Let's look at the drivers from the ACSI model.

Regardless of product, there are three general factors that determine how well a company's offerings correspond to the idiosyncrasy of consumer demand: expectations, quality, and price. Expectations are about prior knowledge. The ACSI data suggest that customer expectations are quite accurate in the aggregate, but also adaptive in the face of changing market conditions. The implication is that aggregate expectations are reasonably well synchronized with the utility products and services actually deliver. Obviously, in the case of repeat purchasing, the consumer relies on previous consumption experiences to form expectations. Unless there is a great variation in quality over time, customer expectations will not be far off the mark.

In the case of first purchase, the situation is different. By definition, the buyer has no personal experience and other sources of information come into play. Advertising and promotion now have a more important role. So do recommendations from other buyers and third-party reviews. Here, too, there are forces balancing expectations. If advertising claims are exaggerated, a long-time customer relationship might be sacrificed in order to get a single sale. If, on the other hand, the seller seeks to create low expectations with the idea that surpassing them will lead to high customer satisfaction, there is a risk of getting no sales at all. In other words, there is a system of "checks and balances" that constrains the seller's incentive to either exaggerate claims or deflate expectations.

Managers often overestimate the importance of customer expectations. Since most purchases are repeat purchases, there is little a seller can do to manage expectations beyond what is reflected in the product or service. Nevertheless, there are cases in which expectations are way off. But they are not very common and they only occur under certain conditions. Let me give an example.

I was having dinner with my wife and daughter. Having grown up in a coastal town near the Baltic Sea, much of what I ate as a youngster came from the sea. Oven-baked cod was a particular favorite. In my youth, cod was an inexpensive fish, but when fresh and prepared by my mother, it made a marvelous meal. Every now and then, my wife Anne would indulge me by serving fresh cod. My daughter Alice was three years old at the time and the two of us were sitting next to one another as Anne served the pale whitish pieces onto our plates. Alice, who had mastered the skills of eating with a knife and fork at an early age, took a bite. She was quiet for a second or two. Then she gave her mother the "stare"—the kind of gaze three-year-olds use when a parent needs to be educated. "This is the worst chicken I have ever tasted," Alice proclaimed.

And so it was. Cod is not chicken, but without previous consumption experience of the former, its color might make the inexperienced diner mistake it for fish. Texture and flavor don't, however. For a toddler, expectations may be off, but not for the rest of us. True, in first-purchase situations, our expectations may be off, but otherwise not—not by much anyway. It is also true that the older we get, the more accurate are our expectations. Older people tend to be more satisfied with their purchases. Individuals 75 years or older have an ACSI score about 10 percent higher than the rest of the population. They are more experienced; they might have a better knowledge of self, a better grasp of budgets, and are probably less likely, in the main, to take risks with new products that they have not tried before.

Also, women are more satisfied than men. This is true for all sectors of the economy and for all countries for which we have analyzed the data. The economic explanation for this is that women, in general, are better buyers than men. They expend more effort shopping and they do it more frequently. The fact that older people and women have higher levels of satisfaction doesn't mean that it would pay to target markets consisting of older women. The cause-and-effect operates in the opposite direction.

In businesses as diverse as personal computers, entertainment media, and information technology, buyers are looking for greater levels of customization. Unless all customers have the same preferences, some degree of customization is necessary. This is different from the general notion of "quality," which is often more about reliability. On the other hand, the value of customization suffers if the product breaks down and the customer needs service. Dell has been through peaks and valleys in this regard: great success in customization followed by serious problems in customer service.

Even though quality and customer satisfaction are closely related, they also differ in important ways. One can be satisfied with something without necessarily believing that it is of high quality. In the fast food business, for example, customer satisfaction is reasonably high— higher than one would expect from looking at quality alone. Customers don't find fast food to be of particularly high quality, but falling prices have contributed to higher satisfaction.

Hyundai and Comcast illustrate how quality and satisfaction can move together in a dramatic fashion, but in opposite directions. Between 1999 and 2004, Hyundai's customer satisfaction improved by 24 percent and quality went up about the same. Comcast went the other direction. When first measured in 2001, it had an ACSI score of 64 and an overall quality score of 73. By 2007, Comcast's quality dropped to 66 and its customer satisfaction score followed, plunging to 56. Quality is a potent, albeit not the most important, predictor of satisfaction.

The third driver of customer satisfaction is related to the buyer's ability to purchase. In addition to our expectations, our previous experience with the quality of the product enables us to make a judgment about the value price paid. Both quality and price affect customer satisfaction. In most cases, quality dominates. The role of price is greater in determining whether or not a purchase is made in the first place. But low price appears to release little dopamine. Once the purchase is made, price matters less than quality. In fact, quality is remembered long after price is forgotten.

Over the past decade we have seen a great deal of price promotion; retailers have dropped prices over the holiday seasons and during other prime selling periods. U.S. car companies have been very active with all sorts of price promotions. Even banks, insurance companies, and fast food restaurants have lowered prices or used price discounting as a means to move products. Yet, it is difficult to find any situation in which improved customer satisfaction has followed. At least not in a major way. But there is another relationship here. The past ten years have witnessed low inflation. Low inflation and low interest rates typically go together. Interest rates have an effect on customer satisfaction. Since satisfied customers represent an economic asset to the seller, that asset will depreciate at a slower pace when interest rates fall. Specifically, the discounted present value of repeat business increases when interest rates drop. Accordingly, low interest rates encourage companies to devote more resources to satisfying customers in the hope they will come back in the future. Rising interest rates have the opposite effect. The discounting of future income will be greater, and the value of a loyal customer goes down.

IN SUM

The science of satisfaction helps us extract information and learn from economics, psychology, and neuroscience in order to strengthen customer relationships. Its application demonstrates:

- that price is a double-edged sword,
- that data must be filtered before it can be put to use,

- that expressing satisfaction quantities in percentages is misleading,
- that the typical scales companies use for measurement don't have enough granularity,
- that common measurement practices generate little information and a lot of noise,
- that measurement must be interpreted within a context,
- that customer satisfaction is similar to finding a good dancing partner, and
- that matching is the most critical element—not quality, not price.

Customer expectations can only be manipulated when customers don't have relevant experience. We may well try to manage the expectations of Wall Street, but the management of customer expectations is a futile task.

Let me add one more element about how we extract information from customers. In most consumer markets, we don't need to go to every single customer for the information. All we need is a sample. If we draw a probability sample (e.g., a random sample), we can generalize what we find to the population of interest. Nielsen Media Research has been taken to task because it no longer calculates "the margin of error" on its ratings.[10] But there is no such thing as "margin of error" without a context. If the confidence level is large enough, I can get to any margin of error you want. I can also reduce my margin of error by increasing the size of my sample.

I often get questions about the ACSI regarding its sample size and margin of error. My answer is that the sample size is about 80,000 per year. "That's big" is the typical comment back. With a confidence level of 90 percent, 0.10 on a 100-point scale in the overall ACSI is usually significant. "Pretty precise, then" is the typical comment back. But the sample size for any individual company is 250. "Really, isn't that too small?" is what I hear back. "What's the margin of error then?" That depends. It's smaller for Heinz than it is for Dell, even at the same level of confidence. This is because the satisfaction scores for Dell have more variation. Once I was asked to determine the sample size for estimating the average wage in a Karl Marx Utopia. Nobody knew what the average wage was, but because Utopialand requires all wages to be equal, my answer was that a sample size of one was all that was needed. Everybody understands that this would be enough. If there is no variation, who needs a sample? But I remember when CFI was bidding for a project comparing customer satisfaction levels for a company with operations in France and China. Our conclusion was that China didn't need to have a larger sample than France, but we lost to a company that recommended a sample size for China that was many times larger than that of France. It is of course true that China has a much larger population than France, but that's not what determines sample size. As soon as one moves away from the obvious, sample size and statistics are not well understood in business. The same is true regarding probability theory. What level of confidence do I need? In most research, 95 percent or even 99 percent are common, but not necessarily appropriate. Such levels might be required if the stakes are high, as in life or death situations. But in business? In a well diversified stock portfolio, I will do well if I bet on the right horse more than 50 percent of the time, assuming a reasonably long time horizon. In business, I might be better off acting on a change in numbers whenever the probability of a change is higher than the probability of no change. This too depends on context. If the risk of doing nothing is high, should the change in numbers be real, something should probably be done. In my experience, it is much better to act on changes even if they may not be statistically significant. Just because something is not statistically significant doesn't mean that status quo prevails. In most cases, the odds are that this is not the case. Unless the cost of taking action is high, it is usually better to treat insignificant changes as potential opportunities or threats, rather than assuming that nothing has changed because of a lack of statistical significance.

CHAPTER 4

When Customer Satisfaction Matters and When It Doesn't

Many companies have consistently created high levels of customer satisfaction include Apple, Amazon, eBay, Wachovia, Kohl's, J.C. Penney, Target, Costco, Publix, VF Corporation, Molson Brewing Company, H.J. Heinz, Clorox, The Hershey Company, Toyota, Google, Southwest Airlines, FedEx, and UPS. For the most part, these companies have outperformed their competition financially, too. But not always. For companies that have not treated their customers well, the opposite is generally true. Most of the airlines fall in this category. Dell, Macy's, Sears Circuit City, Home Depot, Wal-Mart, Levi Strauss, Tyson Foods, Ford, Chrysler, AOL Time Warner, Sprint Nextel, Comcast, and Charter Communications have all faced issues with customer satisfaction at one time or another. Financial difficulties have usually followed.

More than a dozen years of customer satisfaction data have demonstrated a basic truth about market economies: The more powerful the consumers, the more responsive the companies and the higher the resulting customer satisfaction. Markets in which consumers don't have much power tend to have low customer satisfaction. When consumers are empowered by a multitude of choices, ready access to information about those alternatives, and low costs of switching from one company's product to that of a competitor, the customer is king. Companies that fail their customers lose them. Market share erodes and investors leave for greener pastures. For companies in industries where consumers don't have a great deal of choice, where good information is harder to come by, and where the costs associated with rejecting one brand for another are high, customer satisfaction typically suffers.

Yet, high customer satisfaction may not necessarily imply greater revenues and smaller companies may well have more satisfied customers. In the airline industry, ironically, the tragedy of September 11, 2001, created higher levels of passenger satisfaction at a time when most airlines suffered sharp reductions in revenue. What accounted for the gain in satisfaction? The drop in airline travel immediately following September 11, particularly among business travelers, meant less-crowded planes and more time available per passenger from flight attendants. I recall a trip from Detroit to Washington, D.C., in the middle of December 2001 to announce the annual results of the ACSI federal government index. It's a short flight, only a little over an hour, and while perhaps there isn't typically the volume of business traveling between Detroit and D.C. that there is from New York, the route is usually well-traveled. On this occasion, however, there couldn't have been more than 50 people on a plane that carries well over 200. Despite the added layers of security, we passed through the screenings a bit faster than before September 11. The flight attendants were able to complete the beverage service so quickly that they came through with a second round of drinks and snacks. Customer service had improved even though airlines slashed fares and offered a variety of other financial incentives in order to fill seats. In other words, while the airlines didn't take any action to provide more and better services, smaller passenger loads allowed individual travelers to receive better service and discounting meant that service was coming at a lower cost. Loss of customers and, paradoxically, higher levels of customer satisfaction may well go together. It doesn't mean that the consumer suddenly became more powerful in the airline industry nor does it suggest that satisfaction causes customer defection, but rather that customer defection may lead to higher levels of satisfaction among the remaining customers.

The buyer tends to exercise the greatest power over the seller of manufactured goods. At the very top in customer satisfaction are several nondurable goods—food and other frequently purchased products such as soft drinks, beer, personal care products, and processed foods. Durables such as autos and household appliances also have high levels of customer satisfaction.

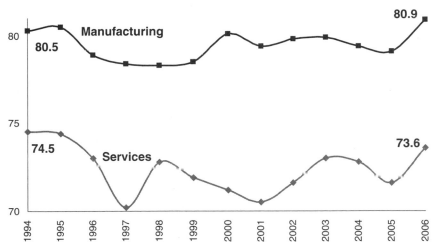

Figure 4.1 ACSI Manufacturing and Services Industries 1994 to 2006

Some service industries are at the opposite end of the scale—among the worst are cable TV, wireless telephone service, and commercial airlines. Competition, many alternatives of choice, low switching costs, high frequency of purchase, good quality control, falling prices, and little need for customer service have all contributed to high levels of satisfaction with nondurables. The soft drink market has the highest satisfaction of any industry. As with other competitive markets, soft drink consumers buy what they like. If dissatisfied with one brand they shift to another. Compared with less frequently purchased goods, this process is very quick—the time from trial to rejection could be measured in seconds. The cost of switching is low. As a result, customer satisfaction *must* be high for soft drink makers to remain competitive. Likewise, the manufacturers of durable goods must maintain high levels of customer satisfaction, but there is one key difference: Switching costs are high, but this is negated somewhat by low purchase frequency. Because I can count on the dishwasher I purchase today to last many years, I don't consider the relatively high cost of buying a different machine as a barrier to switching brands when faced with the next purchase opportunity.

With services, the combination of labor and technology is vital to the buyer-seller relationship, and unlike pure goods, services are *co-produced* by seller and buyer. And because service production involves more human resources by both provider and user, the unpredictability (or variation) in the service production process is greater. Either the store personnel or the customer or both could be having an "off day." On top of that, technologies that must be routinely manipulated by seller and buyer might not always perform as well as intended or expected. Whether it's the cashier, the bank teller, the dry cleaner, the butcher, the baker, or the mocha-latte-double-espresso-with-skim maker, there is an inherent variability to the whole service process that creates challenges for controlling quality. The result is that, on the whole, services have systematically lower levels of customer satisfaction.

But there is another element to consider with respect to some types of services that can have a negative effect on the satisfaction of the buyer: the competitive landscape. There are almost no nondurables goods for frequent or everyday use for which there aren't dozens or more choices. The same cannot be said for services. The landlord is a classic villainous character because he'd be slow to make repairs but quick to raise rents; however, the cost of moving may well be higher than sticking it out. Basic utilities like electric, gas, and telephone services have a long history of somewhat monopolistic behavior. The consumer is all the more captive to poor service in such industries because they are necessities.

Typically, a consumer living in Anytown, U.S.A. has only one electric utility and one cable TV provider, with perhaps a satellite dish as an alternative. These are local monopolies, providing vital services—in the case of energy; most customers have little choice *not* to buy and they have *no* choice when it comes to which firm they're buying it from. As a result, the buyer's power to punish firms that don't provide satisfactory service is very limited. Other industries come with high switching barriers that make it more difficult for dissatisfied customers to go to rival companies: This is the case for wireless telephone service providers and airlines. Here, the buyer may have some power to reward or punish sellers, but that power is weak. Some companies can have low customer satisfaction without having to worry about its effects on sales or profits.

Such companies can chug along, generating strong revenues and healthy profits unless satisfaction falls too low. Cable TV provider Comcast has one of the lowest levels of customer satisfaction in the ACSI but posts a strong financial performance in an industry in which it has little to fear from other cable companies. For retailers, hotels, banks, restaurants, and many other service providers, wherever there is competition and buyers can take their business elsewhere, firms with high customer satisfaction will typically win and those with low satisfaction will struggle. Reinvesting profits in the customer asset lays the groundwork for long-term health. Cutting costs for short-term profits by downsizing frontline staff is risky. Home Depot, Circuit City, and Dell have learned this lesson the hard way.

IT'S ALL ABOUT THE SERVICE (BUT WE'RE GETTING LESS OF IT)

The problem with customer service today is two-fold and paradoxical: In many arenas, the quality of customer service has been declining, while, simultaneously, the economy has become proportionately more and more about services. Just after the end of World War II, services were up barely one-third of total personal consumption expenditures (not including government services). That proportion reached 50 percent in the United States during the early Reagan years and is now close to 60 percent. As the economy produces more services, the quality of service will play a large role in the overall health of the economy. More than a decade ago, some were heralding the death of customer service.

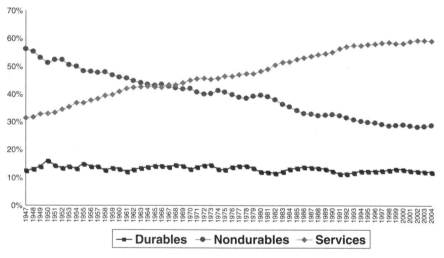

Figure 4.2 U.S. Personal Consumption Expenditures 1947 to 2004

That may be an overstatement, but service quality in some industries was problematic. Everyone has a horror story to tell about service. What matters is whether such experiences are becoming more or less frequent. Is the quality of both goods and services improving or declining? What are customers' expectations of the products and services they buy? Do they change over time? What about value for money? How do changes in price affect satisfaction? When I began the ACSI in 1994, we established a baseline for customer satisfaction from which to evaluate future changes. The rapid pace at which labor was replaced by technology had more impact on service industries than manufacturing, and customer satisfaction declined sharply between 1994 and 1996. After 1997, customer satisfaction began to recover, as the economy grew at a faster rate and companies devoted more resources to servicing demand. Satisfaction fell again four straight quarters during the 2000–2001 recession, but has since followed a mostly upward trajectory, dropping significantly in only one other period, at the end of 2004 and beginning of 2005.

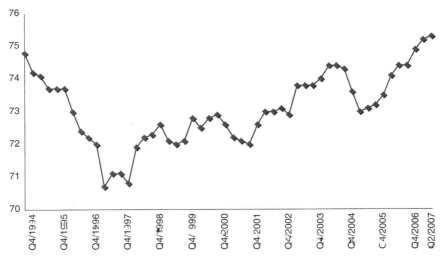

Figure 4.3 ACSI 1994 to Q2 2007

Source: American Customer Satisfaction Index

In 2007, the ACSI was at a record high. This may be surprising to those who continue to encounter service deficiencies. It is clear that many service problems remain, but the past decade also has been an extraordinary period of low inflation and product innovation, while customers have also managed to adjust to some of the new technologies that involve less labor.

THE CHALLENGES OF A SELF-SERVICE ECONOMY

The idea of shifting greater responsibility for service from the seller to the buyer was not unique in the 1990s, but the pace at which it was occurring was faster. Corporate downsizing and a wave of new service technologies combined to dampen satisfaction, with the ACSI falling 5 percent from 1994 to 1996. As customers struggle to learn new service technologies, satisfaction tends to suffer in the short term. Users often become frustrated initially both by the new technologies and the lack of service personnel. Instead of having trained staff ready to help with service needs, buyers now do a good deal of what bank tellers, cashiers, gas station attendants, and ticket agents used to do. From ATMs at nearly every major intersection to toll-free help lines and automatic checkouts, we may soon reach the limit of the "self-service" economy. Off-loading work onto the buyer puts greater demands on buyers' increasingly scarce time resources.

Gas stations, sometimes more formally called gasoline service stations (when "service" meant just that), are a case in point. In the 1950s, attendants pumped gasoline, checked the oil and tire pressure, and cleaned the windshield. In the 1985 film *Back to the Future*, after Michael J. Fox's character Marty is transported back to the year 1955, one of the first visual images that seems out of place to him is that of a car pulling into a Texaco station where several red-capped attendants rush out to service the car. This was all but unheard of in the film's present day of 1985. Then, as now, self-service was the rule at gas stations: We pump our own gas, often handling the financial transaction ourselves by paying at the pump with a credit card, and if the windshield is dirty, there's a squeegee sitting in a bucket of wiper solution.

Self-service at gas stations is actually prohibited by law in two states, New Jersey and Oregon, on environmental grounds. These states' argument against self-service is that customers are not sufficiently skilled at the task of pumping gas. Fuel may spill and damage the environment. But even in these two states, full service has been replaced by "mini-service"—the gas is pumped by an attendant; if you want a clean windshield or need air for a sagging tire, you're on your own. Today, with the task of pumping gas now almost exclusively the responsibility of the buyer, satisfaction with gas stations is largely dependent on price. Gasoline is one of the very few consumer industries where price matters more than quality—gasoline is gasoline and there is little differentiation among sellers. What matters is how fast the dollars are dialing by on the pump. It's no surprise then that the customer satisfaction ups and downs of the industry over the years have tracked with fluctuations in gasoline prices. But, even here, time may matter. Not just how fast the dollars amass on the pump, but how fast drivers get in and out.

YOU EXPECT ME TO DO THIS MYSELF?

As we have become accustomed to servicing our own cars at gas stations, this form of self-service is now largely taken for granted. The process is simple and easily mastered: Swipe your credit card, choose the grade of gas, pump the amount you want, take your receipt. A more recent and, it seems, frustrating self-service technology is the self-checkout machines in retail stores, most popular today in the larger supermarket chains and some big-box retailers. The machines are designed to accomplish the two-fold benefit necessary for success: (1) convenience to the customer through greater efficiency and (2) cost savings to the retailer due to eliminating of labor. Services like bagging or carting groceries to the parking lot used to be provided by the seller. Typically, this work is now done by the buyers. But here, there is no clear benefit to the buyer.

While it is easy to argue that self-checkout lanes help accomplish the second goal of reducing labor cost, it is not apparent that they accomplish the first goal. Are they better for the customer? Here, the learning curve is longer than self-service at the gasoline pump, with the customer having to scan dozens of different pieces of merchandise, some of it, such as fresh produce, requiring multi-digit codes to be looked up and the items weighed. I recall without fondness my first handful of experiences at the grocery self-checkout—fumbling with food items, looking for the barcode, finally locating it, and still having to swipe the item several times across the scanner to get it to read the code while the line of customers behind me grew. When finally done, the machine instructed me to "please place the item *back* in the bag," which is where it was already. All in all, it seemed that the lines got longer—not shorter. Self checkouts require at least some level of know-how, a familiarity with a range of merchandise that cashiers are trained to have. And while a cashier who is ill-equipped for the job and causes congestion can be re-trained or re-deployed or let go, there is no protection against the trouble created by an inexperienced customer. Research findings[1] suggest that the result is often longer lines and longer wait times, contrary to what the system is designed to accomplish.

Troublesome as this might seem, there has been no discernable effect on customer satisfaction. The supermarket ACSI scores have been quite stable over the past few years. Why hasn't the introduction of these machines and customers' generally negative reaction to them had a measurable effect on customer satisfaction? First, there is much more that goes into customers' overall satisfaction with a supermarket experience than the checkout process. Variety and inventory of merchandise, cleanliness of the store, parking, prices, and convenience matter more. Also, unlike gas stations, where self-service is the rule, supermarkets and other retailers have not (yet) replaced cashiers entirely. Self-checkout is an option alongside traditional, albeit fewer, checkout lanes. Buyers are still offered choice. Unless the consumer cost of choosing is too high, having choice is usually better than not having it. That's lesson one. The other lesson is that even though most consumers don't like the automatic checkouts, the marginal effect of eliminating or fixing them is small. Just because customers say they don't like something doesn't mean that it has a strong effect on their satisfaction. Ultimately, time will sort out who's going to perform the checkout service—if self-checkouts increase the cost of shopping time for consumers, buyers will demand that the seller provide checkout service (and they might pay for it, too).

Not all efficiencies introduced via new self-service technologies cause frustrations and some have had an immediate impact for the better. Self-service check-in for air travel, whether from one's home or office computer, or at kiosks at the airport, are working well. Boarding passes can be printed from the office before leaving for the airport, avoiding lines at the ticket counter. When we go online, it may be possible to change or upgrade seats. Even better, if it's a short trip, with a return in less than 24 hours, boarding passes for the return flight can be printed too. Whether accessed from the comfort of one's own home, office, or from an easy-to-use computer kiosk at the airport, this is an example of an innovation that saves time for buyers and reduces cost for sellers.

THE SMALL TOWN STORE THAT ISN'T SO SMALL

In Ann Arbor, Michigan, as in any medium-sized U.S. city, there is no shortage of retailers offering a wide selection of food and other grocery items, from the largest national and regional supermarket chains such as Kroger, of which there are six serving the Ann Arbor population of about 120,000, to individual "mom-and-pop" stores selling produce, ethnic groceries, cheese, and wine. Conventional wisdom has always held that the smaller the store, the better the service. The ideal of years gone by is the little shop where, like the *Cheers* bar, everybody knows your name. As much as I like to prove conventional wisdom wrong, in this case, it's not. Year after year of ACSI data show that, in general, smaller companies do better by the customer than their larger competitors. Among hotel chains, fast-food franchises, airlines, drug stores, banks, and supermarkets, smaller firms consistently achieve higher levels of satisfaction than their industry averages and, in some cases, outperform all of the well-known, larger companies. For example, none of the big three drug-store chains, CVS, Rite Aid, or Walgreens, can match the smaller drug stores in satisfaction. Smaller airlines beat every big carrier with the exception of Southwest, while smaller supermarkets top every chain but Publix. These smaller competitors are by no means "mom-and-pop" companies. Many of them are rather large regional chains. No one would suggest that SunTrust Bank or Popeye's Chicken are businesses where everybody knows your name, but by-and-large even these medium-size companies do a better job at satisfying their customers than their larger counterparts. And, if they couldn't, they would be out of business. It's not that smaller companies do better by their customers by default. Because they usually can't compete on price, they have no choice: They must compete on service and customer satisfaction.

One important factor in keeping satisfaction high for the small to mid-size firm has to do with maintaining a "small feel" even as it grows. The grocery chain Trader Joe's, which made Ann Arbor one of its five Michigan locations a couple of years ago, is a good example. When the local Whole Foods, another fast-growing grocery chain, moved into larger facilities about a mile away, Trader Joe's took over the old store, adhering to one of the many successful pieces of the company's business model—moving into abandoned retail locations to set up shop at lower cost. Trader Joe's is self-described as "your unique grocery store." Starting out as a local chain in Southern California, where most of its stores are still located, the company has expanded to around 250 stores in 23 states. As a privately held company owned by the German discount giant ALDI, estimates put Trader Joe's 2006 sales at about $5 billion, just slightly below Whole Foods. The stores are not very large and the range of merchandise is not as broad as a typical supermarket. There are few national brands and a fairly limited selection of meat and produce. What Trader Joe's does well is provide a variety of frozen foods, gourmet and organic products, and other types of dry goods, more than 70 percent of which carry the store's own brand name, at relatively low prices.

Trader Joe's is obviously not unique in offering a slew of company-branded products in certain niche categories at affordable prices. What makes it stand out among supermarkets is its emphasis on traditional notions of customer service, based on well-trained, highly motivated employees. Trader Joe's staff is not unionized but is paid above-average wages and bonuses. It also contributes 15 percent of gross wages to a funded retirement plan. I hadn't been to Trader Joe's until recently, but the director of the ACSI, David VanAmburg, and his wife shop there regularly and one day over lunch he told me why.

He remarked on how the store bends over backward to provide great service. I was curious about how different Trader Joe's might be from other grocery stores. Browsing up and down the aisles in search of cookies for one, according to David. Unable to find them, he noticed an employee stocking canned goods, and asked for help, expecting to be told in which aisle to find them. Instead, the employee stopped what he was doing and took David directly to the cookies. "He could have just told me where to look," David said to me. "I thought it was impressive that he actually took me there." Apparently, it's store policy to take customers to exactly where the item in question is located. Employees are not allowed merely to tell customers where to look.

To this, the employee replied that it's store policy to take customers to exactly where the item in question is located. Employees are not allowed merely to tell customers where to look.

David then explained another Trader Joe's approach to customer service: its return policy. We expect to be able to return damaged or spoiled merchandise for replacement or full refund, no surprise there, but how about food that you have tried and just didn't care for? Trader Joe's has a business model that seeks to encourage a broad sampling of its branded products and with the idea that you will find something to like that the store is willing to refund products the consumer tries and simply doesn't like. I had thought this was unique to non-rival goods. But at Trader Joe's you can apparently eat your cake and return it, too. Trader Joe's turns dissatisfaction with new product trials into opportunities to strengthen customer loyalty to the store. Don't like a product? Here's your money back and we hope you will try something else. The approach seems to work. Sales per store square foot are nearly twice that of typical supermarkets, and as Trader Joe's increased its number of stores fivefold between 1990 and 2001, profits grew tenfold.

THE NOT-SO-FRIENDLY SKIES

The ease and speed with which consumers can reject one product in favor of another is restricted in the airline business. Because there is no easy way out once in the air, passengers can be tormented longer than in other business. Even on the ground, it turns out. I remember being stuck on the airport tarmac after landing with no food or water, overflowing toilets, and screaming passengers for a whole day. Some airport employees had not shown up for work that morning because of a severe snowstorm. But what was worse was the breakdown in communications as the airline failed to resolve the problem. The incident was eventually settled in a class-action lawsuit. It's usually not a good idea to get into legal disputes with your customers. It would probably have been much less costly to compensate passengers well before going to court. The airline in question, Northwest, encountered many other service breakdowns and customer satisfaction took a big hit, with scores plummeting 16 percent to a record low.

Because many airports in the United States are controlled by a few carriers, passenger choice is limited. As a resident of southeast

Michigan, Northwest is by default the airline of choice. It flies to many destinations. I could pick another airline, but there are fewer flights to choose from and many have connections. Major airlines also engage in aggressive pricing at their hubs to keep smaller carriers away. The scenario is almost always the same: A smaller carrier like Spirit or Jet Blue enters a hub offering low-priced fares to select destinations. The larger carrier either undercuts the discounter's price to those destinations and adds more flights or, if it does not offer a flight to one or more of those destinations, it begins to do so. This kind of pressure used to drive the smaller competitor away, but not anymore. The major airlines have been so weakened by increasing fuel costs, labor challenges, and high fixed costs that they have become much more vulnerable to low-price competition. Most of them have also cut costs. Under these conditions, it is not easy to improve customer service, especially when the cost-cutting is directed at labor. Consequently, it is not surprising that airlines have been among the lowest in customer satisfaction. Between 1994 and 2000, the airline ACSI score fell by more than 12 percent and the problems have gotten worse.

But there are exceptions. Southwest Airlines has shown that it is possible to achieve high levels of passenger satisfaction and to be profitable. Southwest's market value is now greater than all other U.S. airlines combined. The Southwest approach has always been to offer a basic, slimmed-down service and to be good at it: consistently deliver passengers on time to their destination also with luggage. Most other airlines have difficulty doing this, especially combining the movement of passengers and their luggage. But Southwest does it at low cost and low price.

Unlike the other major carriers, tickets must be bought directly from Southwest, rather than through travel agents or Internet travel sites like Expedia and Travelocity. But tickets can be changed without penalty. There is no assigned seating and no food prepared in flight; passengers may take whatever open seat is available and are given a "snack pack" upon boarding longer flights. While Southwest has scaled back on some of the traditional comforts of flying in return for lower ticket prices and friendly staff, it has always topped the airline industry in customer satisfaction. It has bested the industry average by 12 percent; in no other business has a company consistently outperformed its competition by such a wide margin.

WHEN RELIABILITY IS THE ISSUE

Like airlines, cable and satellite TV have faced a good deal of customer dissatisfaction over the years. Heavy system loads, reliability problems, and an emphasis on technology investment at the expense of customer service are traits cable companies share with airlines. They also share some degree of monopoly power. Cable companies have focused largely on two types of investments: mergers and acquisitions to increase market share, and technology upgrades to offer more television channels and faster Internet access. Comcast has been successful at both. It became the largest cable and high-speed Internet service provider in the United States through a series of acquisitions, culminating in 2001 with its purchase of AT&T Broadband, then the largest U.S. cable company. In 2006 Comcast and Time Warner Cable agreed to divide Adelphia Cable, the fifth-largest cable company before it filed for bankruptcy in 2002.

Comcast has based its promotional thrust on two central themes. One is the superiority of cable over satellite TV: Its ads depict a woeful, former satellite customer spinning tales of horrible experiences with satellite dishes. Either the dish blew off the roof, the picture turned to static when it rained, or getting a clear picture depended on someone holding the dish in a certain way, as in the early days of television when antennas were needed. But just as it's not a good idea to get into litigation with customers, it's not wise to allege superiority when customers see none. Ever since the cable/satellite business was added to the ACSI in 2001, the two satellite providers, DirecTV and Dish Network, have outperformed all cable operators combined. This is not to suggest that satellite TV is doing particularly well by its customers either, but the consistency by which they do better than cable is noteworthy. Satellite TV ACSI scores hover around 70, while cable TV scores remain as much as 10 percent below.

Comcast's other advertising theme is about its offerings: more cable channels and new features (such as its own TiVo-like recording capability, and *faster* Internet access); web pages that appear and refresh quicker; and downloads that take less time (up to twice as fast as before). Although the value of consumer discretionary time is increasing because its supply is shrinking, customer satisfaction is about more than time savings. Consumers do want faster services, but not at the expense of quality. Reliability will trump speed every time. A cable provider can promise downloading a gigantic data file in a nanosecond, but if the cable connection is down, what is the point?

High system load is one of the major culprits. Cable companies promote more offerings and greater speed in order to attract more subscribers, both of which tax the system unless it is expanded and upgraded. The greater the number of subscribers, the less reliable the system tends to be, and the more customers per service person, the worse the service tends to be. But, profitability in the cable business doesn't hinge on customer satisfaction. One might argue that cable companies are, in effect, rational by not squandering precious resources on customer service. Better to increase price. Basic cable services in the United States rose 5 percent in 2006 and 93 percent during the past decade, almost 400 percent more than the rate of increase in overall consumer prices.[2] Poor service and high prices are usually associated with monopolies. Only in a few, mostly large, metropolitan areas is there more than one cable TV operator. For many households, there is no choice. Renters and homeowners in condominium communities are often prohibited by association rules from having satellite dishes.

No wonder that customer satisfaction is low in the cable TV business. Lower than that of the IRS. That doesn't mean that people enjoy paying taxes more than they do watching cable TV, but in the context of what these organizations do, the former offers a more satisfactory experience than the latter. In most competitive situations, such low scores wouldn't be sustainable: Either firms improve or they are forced out of business. Things are different for cable TV. Whereas many industries lack pricing power, that's not true of cable. The dissatisfied customer cannot inflict much financial punishment on cable companies because there is nowhere else to go. With monopoly power comes monopoly profits.

As customer satisfaction has sagged, revenues and profits soared. Comcast posted its lowest customer satisfaction in five years in 2007, after finishing the prior year with a 175 percent increase in net income and a 50 percent surge in stock price. In the first quarter of 2007 alone, Comcast added 75,000 new cable TV subscribers, a 49 percent increase, leading to an 80 percent rise in earnings over the previous first quarter.

CAN YOU HEAR ME NOW?

Like cable TV, wireless telephone service has generally done well financially despite low customer satisfaction. Network coverage, dropped calls, and reliability problems, coupled with high switching barriers, have kept customer satisfaction at basement levels in the ACSI. But things might be changing. An easing of switching barriers has created more buyer leverage, wireless providers have responded by providing better service and satisfaction has improved. It used to be that one had to give up one's telephone number, and often the phone itself, in order to switch supplier. That barrier has been eliminated. But the service contract remains. If a subscriber wants to cancel before the contract expires, the cancellation fee can be $50 to $200; effectively locking in customers, but detrimental to customer satisfaction and (probably) to long-term profitability. When switching barriers come down, and they eventually will customers leave. The U.S. Federal Communications Commission eased the problem of transferring phone numbers when it mandated number portability for all cellular service, and customer satisfaction has risen by 8 percent since. As consumers become more empowered, they have also doled out more financial punishment. Sprint Nextel is a case in point. The company is the number three U.S. wireless provider and has battled tough financial times before. Satisfaction with its wireless business was among the lowest in the industry and to combat weakening demand for its wireless products, Sprint made large labor cuts—some 22,000 jobs in 2003 and 2004. Then, in response to the shrinking business, Sprint acquired new customers in a $35 billion merger with Nextel: a net gain of 16 million subscribers. But buying customers doesn't come without obligations: Now they have to be serviced. In this case, the new subscribers didn't come without liability—Nextel's customer satisfaction was even lower than Sprint's. Add one group of dissatisfied customers to another and what do we get? Adding two negatives doesn't make a positive. What Sprint Nextel got was a large group of unhappy subscribers. It's difficult enough to get mergers to work out well—and most don't—but when a company with unhappy customers acquires a company with even more unhappy customers, it's difficult to get a good outcome.

Sprint's difficulties have persisted. While customer satisfaction in the industry as a whole has improved, Sprint has gone in the opposite direction. Customer satisfaction has plunged to 10 percent below competition in 2007. Customers have left and financials have taken a beating. More than 300,000 premium subscribers canceled service in the fourth quarter of 2006 alone, and the company's share price fell 20 percent. In fact, Sprint's satisfaction dropped to such a low level that customers have become more willing to pay the canceling fee. When a protective switching barrier becomes porous, investors are likely to depart as well. That's the risk Sprint Nextel is facing.

GIANTS WITH LITTLE CUSTOMER SATISFACTION, BUT STILL DOING WELL

Aside from Comcast, there are other companies that may do well financially—but for different reasons—despite low customer satisfaction. Wal-Mart and McDonald's are in this category, although the former has had more challenges of late. Both are market-share leaders with customer satisfaction scores consistently anchored at the bottom of their respective industries. While Comcast can do well because it has considerable local monopoly power, that's not exactly the case for Wal-Mart or for McDonald's, at least not in the same sense.

Let's take McDonald's first. Its Golden Arches are the most recognizable image of fast food not only in the United States but throughout the world, and the name is so ubiquitous that it has given rise to "McWords," cultural buzzwords that are sometimes pejorative: "McJob" (a low-paying, unskilled employment of any kind), and "McMajor" (a college major likely to lead nowhere but a "McJob"), but also, as on the popular television drama *Grey's Anatomy*, "McDreamy" and "McSteamy." From a small franchise establishment purchased by Ray Kroc in the 1950s that served thousands, McDonald's now serves millions. Chicken nuggets, breakfast foods, salads, "super sizing," and many other innovations in the fast-food industry have come from McDonald's. But despite introducing product innovations and consistently being the strongest brand in the fast-food business, McDonald's has never reached the fast-food industry average in customer satisfaction. Even as the fast-food business as a whole has slowly improved the satisfaction of its customers, McDonald's stood still. While pricing has always been competitive, quality, according to McDonald's own customers, both in terms of service and food, lags. Why is it that McDonald's has such low levels of customer satisfaction? The answer is that it doesn't need satisfied customers to the same extent as its competitors do. McDonald's U.S. revenues alone are larger than the next four largest fast-food chains combined (Burger King, Wendy's, KFC, and Taco Bell). Profits have been good as well, with almost 60 percent growth in net income between 2004 and 2006 and a stock that gained almost 70 percent during that same period.

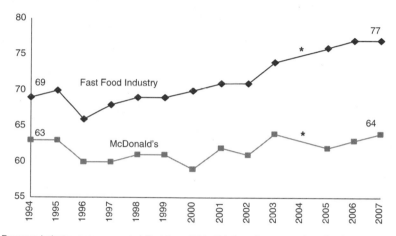

* Because industry measurement shifted from Q4 to Q1, there is no score for calendar year 2004

Figure 4.4 McTroubles? Apparently Not

Source: American Customer Satisfaction Index

There is no real monopoly-type power here. There is an abundance of other fast-food alternatives, often within close distance of the closest McDonald's franchise. If not satisfaction, what keeps customers coming back to McDonald's? In addition to the fact that small children make up a sizeable portion of the customer base, most customers don't go to McDonald's to have a great dining experience. Okay would be enough. Consistency is important. So too are prices that fit lower-income family budgets even though the cost of a typical McDonald's meal or sandwich, fries, and drink is no less than most of the other major fast-food chains. But if we were to survey the under-12 set, McDonald's might well earn the most gold stars. These customers don't care much about prices. They go to McDonald's for the experience—the Happy Meals, the play places with crawl tubes and ball pits to romp around in, the lure of Mayor McCheese, the Hamburglar, and, of course, Ronald McDonald himself. Think McDonald's and think kid-friendly—it's the largest operator of playgrounds in the United States and it is estimated that 90 percent of all children between three and nine go to a McDonald's at least once per month.[3] Add up the number of kids in the United States in that age category, multiply by 12, and then by .90. Now multiply by the average price of a meal, and the revenue is enormous. Now, consider Burger King, Wendy's, Taco Bell, and KFC. Most lack an identifiable kid-appealing "mascot," let alone the range of activities that attract kids. Burger King tried with its "Burger King Kingdom," but that never caught on and was phased out by the late 1980s, leaving only the Burger King himself as the brand's image. But while young children consume, they're not really "customers." It's their parents who pay and who respond to the surveys. McDonald's continues to outsell competition, and it's the families with young children that put it there.

For Wal-Mart there's a different kind of customer demographic at work. Wal-Mart competes in two retail categories: department/discount stores and supermarkets. Wal-Mart Super Centers now sell more groceries than anybody else. In both categories, customer satisfaction is low. A big part of Wal-Mart's business model is based on offering the lowest price in town. The company consistently leads in "value for money," both in the grocery business and in retail merchandising. The ACSI measure of lower in quality and customer service along with weak customer satisfaction are not enough to keep customers from coming back. If the Wal-Mart shopping experience is so underwhelming relative to other retailers, how can price consistently trump quality? For most companies, it's the other way around. Quality has a much greater impact on repeat business than price. What keeps Wal-Mart customers coming back even though they're not very satisfied? Well, they simply don't have much choice. Wal-Mart has such pricing power over its suppliers that it has created something of a demographic segment monopoly. Low-income households are more price sensitive and this is the core constituency of Wal-Mart. It is also true, however, that a majority of all U.S. households shop at Wal-Mart at least once per year. But Wal-Mart's most frequent shoppers—the core of any retailer's customer base from which most earnings are generated—are low-income households. Twenty percent of these consumers don't have bank accounts, more than twice the national average. The "lowest price in town" makes it difficult for low-income households to go elsewhere. It's not so much that price trumps satisfaction, but that household budget constraints do.

Yet, even Wal-Mart may have hit its limit. Like Sprint, customer satisfaction may have dropped too far or remained low for too long so that it's finally starting to show up in the financials. Growth has slowed considerably: In 2000, only 17 percent of all Wal-Mart Super Centers were five years or older; that proportion grew to 44 percent by 2006. Stock price has slumped, falling nearly 30 percent since its all-time high at the beginning of 2000. And the cost of replacing labor is also affecting the company. The average pay at Wal-Mart is $10 an hour. Costco, a competitor and a leader in customer satisfaction, pays $17 an hour. High employee satisfaction is usually associated with strong customer satisfaction. Even though Wal-Mart is saving considerably by paying its workers less, much of those savings are offset by the cost of hiring and training new employees—turnover at Costco is 17 percent, compared to 44 percent at Wal-Mart.[4] Higher staff turnover also has implications, usually negative, for customer satisfaction.

There's another challenge in building a business around a mantra of "always low prices"—it is difficult to have much of an identity beyond price positioning. Competitors such as Target and Kmart have managed to move away somewhat from such an identity—no doubt due to Wal-Mart's pricing—and sought other identities with more exclusive product lines, especially in clothes and furniture. While Wal-Mart may have a strong hold on the lower income customer segment, middle- and higher-end segments are attracted more by product quality, merchandising, and customer service. Price plays an important role, but not to the same extent. And Wal-Mart has trailed competition on everything but price: merchandise quality, selection and inventory, customer service, even the cleanliness and attractiveness of the stores themselves. As long as other discounters played Wal-Mart's pricing game, it had a strong competitive advantage, but with other retailers now differentiating in terms of quality and exclusivity, it's becoming more of a challenge for Wal-Mart to compete on price alone in segments other than low income. Wal-Mart seems to have recognized this, but an early effort in developing its own line of fashion clothing by designer Mark Eisen fell flat in 2007.[5]

SEPARATING WINNERS FROM LOSERS

Even though overall customer satisfaction in the United States has been on the upswing because of increasing competition and consumer empowerment, there is still much room for improvement. While it is not true for all companies, most will find it necessary to improve. For a few, it doesn't matter and it might not pay dividends to have more satisfied customers. Energy utilities, airlines, cable TV, and cell phone service providers are still in this category. As of now, nobody here has outstanding customer satisfaction. Tomorrow will be different, however. As I discussed earlier, predicting the future is not all that difficult. Most of it is an extension of the past. But in this case, the forces that are shaping the future all point toward more competition and more buyer choice. Switching barriers are likely to go the way of the Berlin Wall and those companies that have ignored customer service will have weakened defenses against competitive inroads. For many other companies, particularly in sectors such as retail, finance, durable goods, and sports, high levels of satisfaction are critical to financial well-being. In these industries, buyers wield greater power to reward and punish as they see fit. Punishment is what the Florida Marlins got.

On October 26, 1997, Florida Marlins shortstop Edgar Renteria stepped up to the plate with the bases loaded and two outs in the bottom of the eleventh inning. This wasn't just any extra inning of any game, but the seventh and deciding game of the World Series between the Marlins and the Cleveland Indians at Joe Robbie stadium in Miami before a full-house of 67,204 fans. The underdog Marlins had tied the game at 2–2 with a run in the bottom of the ninth to send it to extra innings, and seldom had there been a more dramatic moment in Series history. The game and the championship were now on the line in a single at bat. Indians pitcher Charles Nagy fired his first offering over the plate: "strike one!" But Renteria found the next pitch to his liking and bounced it high over Nagy's head into center field for the game and Series-winning hit. The Marlins, an expansion team added to the National League only four years earlier, became the youngest franchise and the first ever wild-card team to win the World Series.

The Marlins had their first-ever winning season in 1997, finishing 92–70, nine games behind the division-winning Atlanta Braves, but still good enough for a post-season berth. Blockbuster Video CEO and Miami Dolphins owner Wayne Huizenga had been awarded the expansion franchise that brought Major League baseball to south Florida for the first time and quickly moved to beef up the team's payroll in order to build a winning franchise. The signing of several veteran talents paved the way for the success of 1997, but also brought with it a huge payroll, more than $47 million that year. The World Series celebrations throughout the Miami area had barely begun to tail off when Huizenga, citing financial losses, decided that he would have to dramatically cut costs. The question was, however, where to cut? If there is one constant mistake that companies seem to make over and over, it's cutting costs in the wrong places. Over the winter and into the early part of the 1998 season, the Marlins held what in the world of professional sports is called a "fire sale," trading off some of its highest paid players in exchange for draft picks and prospects with little experience. The Marlins cut their payroll by 30 percent between 1997 and 1998 and further cost-cutting brought the 1999 payroll down to a mere $15 million, less than one-third the payroll of the championship team.

Now it's almost exactly a year later, September 27, 1998. Playing the Philadelphia Phillies, the team made a couple of mistakes that led to four unearned runs in a 7–3 loss, the Marlin's final game of the season and 108th loss of the year. World Series hero Edgar Renteria wasn't in the line-up for the final game but was still part of the team, one of the few regulars still remaining from a year before. Their 54–108 record was the worst in the National League and brought the Marlins another, albeit dubious, "first"—first team to win a World Series followed by a season of 100 or more losses. Fans and media derided Huizenga's "fire sale" and one creative fan got some mileage out of the sarcastic slogan "Wait 'til *last* year!" But from a business point of view, here's the kicker: Attendance fell from 2.4 million in the championship year to 1.7 million the next year, a 27 percent decline that basically mirrored the percentage drop in team payroll. Attendance would fall again in 1999 to 1.4 million, a 42 percent decline compared with 1997. Worse, when past mistakes are corrected, the effects on customer relationships may take a long time. By 2002, the Marlins finished with one of their best records since the 1997 championship, yet they drew a Major League low 800,000 fans to the ballpark. In 2003, they won the World Series but drew 400,000 fewer fans than they had during the 1998 108-loss season.

Marlins ownership took one of the most traveled routes to improving company financial performance quickly: cutting the cost of labor. In the case of a baseball team, you don't reduce the actual number of ballplayers, just as you don't play a piece written for a string quartet with three musicians. But you can swap high-cost labor with low-cost replacements, and this is of course what they did. By reducing labor costs, the Marlins also reduced the quality of the product on the field. Number of wins plummeted and the fan base, clearly dissatisfied, lost faith. Ticket sales fell. Declining satisfaction with the Marlins team meant loss of revenue that future wins would take much longer to restore.

While the Florida Marlins may have taken more drastic action than most to reduce costs in an effort to improve profits, there are many examples where the result impacts revenues to such an extent that the result is a further loss of profit. Cost reductions in a service economy are especially difficult. The principle, however, is simple. You cut costs in activities that have the least marginal effect on customer satisfaction. This has nothing to do per se with what services customers consider important. Now, this is a difficult concept for many to understand. My advice would be to think in a way that most managers analyze the additional cost implications of a new program, activity, or product. In the same way that they would try to figure out what the marginal cost is—that extra cost that we would incur from changing something—we should also try to figure out what the *marginal* effect on customer satisfaction would be for the contemplated cost reduction. Simply thinking in these terms would be a big improvement. But in order to really do it well, we need to have good measures of customer satisfaction and good estimates of what the effect of a change in service would be. If not, we will learn it the hard way. Take electronics retailer Circuit City. The company is a giant in the retail business. With $11 billion of annual sales, Circuit City ranks just behind Wal-Mart and Best Buy in electronics retail sales, a long way from its humble beginnings in the 1950s as Sam Wurtzel's Wards Company, a TV and appliances store in Richmond, Virginia. By 1984, the company had grown rapidly, had a change of name, and became publicly traded. By the turn of this century, Circuit City was well entrenched in the Fortune 200. Several major quality initiatives seemed to pay off handsomely. Investments in multi-channel integration placed the customer asset front and center. Kiosks for customers to order out-of-stock products online were set up, call centers and websites were improved, as was the supply-chain organization for aligning merchandise inventory with customer demand. Taking a cue from other big-box retailers such as Home Depot and Lowe's, the company also rolled out a new installation service dubbed "firedog" in 2006, providing in-store, in-home, and online PC services, home theater installations, and other electronics installation and maintenance services.

Sounds like a good recipe for increasing the value of customer asset, right? But not everybody would see it that way. Accounting didn't. Wall Street often misses the point as well. Since many investments of this kind are not capitalized over time (even though they should be), short-term profits suffer and the pressure from shareholders to change course can be formidable even though the short-term losses may well be an accounting mirage. Circuit City management caved. It slashed costs by laying off 3,900 sales associates, almost 10 percent of its total workforce in 2003. That saved the company about $130 million. But the price was high: a loss of satisfied customers, less repeat business, shrinking revenue, and even more pressure from investors to cut more cost. Customer satisfaction has dropped by 6 percent since. For Best Buy, Circuit City's closest competitor, customer satisfaction rose by 6 percent. Circuit City losses followed. $16 million in the third quarter of 2006. The vicious circle continues. More than 60 stores, about 10 percent of the total, were slated for closure in Canada and the United States in 2007. In fact, on March 28, 2007, Circuit City announced yet another big layoff, this round involving some 3,400 employees, a move designed to reduce costs by $110 million in 2007 and save another $140 million in 2008. Finally, management made its next move right out of the Florida Marlins' playbook, laying off its highest-paid salespeople with plans to replace them with lower-paid workers. In other words, Circuit City didn't trim the volume of its workforce so much as it lowered the quality of that workforce. In a gesture to the fired employees, the company allowed those laid off to reapply for their old jobs but at much lower pay.

Sometimes cost cutting changes the culture of a company—but not always for the better. Little could the owners of Handy Dan have known what they were unleashing when they fired Bernie Marcus and Arthur Blank from their leadership positions at the small California home improvement retailer in 1978. Marcus and Blank started the very next day with plans for a new home improvement company they could mold with their own vision of a corporate culture. Debuting in Atlanta, the first Home Depot quickly grew into a billion-dollar business. By 1997, it was opening its 500th store in the United States and topping $20 billion in sales. By 2000, the number of stores had doubled, as had revenues: Home Depot reached $40 billion in sales at a faster pace than any other retailer had in the past. This was long after Handy Dan went out of business. The big-box retailer with the distinctive orange box logo thrived on founders Marcus and Blank's vision of a customer-centric organization. A combination of superior customer service and low prices proved a recipe for phenomenal success. The management structure allowed considerable autonomy and innovation and encouraged personal initiative with little corporate interference and not much bureaucracy: Store managers could spend a good deal of time with customers, whom they relied upon to get new ideas on how to improve stores. Unwanted corporate paperwork got a "B.S." stamp by store managers and was returned to sender.

But things were about to change at Home Depot. At the end of 2000, a new CEO was hired. Robert Nardelli, a top executive under Jack Welch at General Electric did a complete about-face restructuring of how the company was run. Instead of autonomy, there was now command and control. Operations relied on military practice even to the point of hiring former military personnel. There were 17,000 military veterans employed in 2005, an increase of 70 percent compared with a few years earlier. Some argued that the military was a bad fit for a service business. The military is trained to kill people, not to provide great service, they said. Labor costs were reduced. Home Depot's management structure was overhauled, operations were streamlined, consolidated, and centralized, and discipline was tightened. Nardelli's arrival was not just a tweak of an existing framework; it led to a radical shift in Home Depot's organizational culture, with a shift away from flexibility toward a much more hierarchical organization. Every aspect of Home Depot's operations was now managed and measured with metrics, including the gross margin per labor-hour and the number of "greets" at store entrances. Customer satisfaction was measured, but not much attention seemed to be paid to it.

As is often the case, Wall Street didn't see what was coming. Analysts were excited by the new direction, lauding the "command-and-control" approach. And the short-term results were not bad. Home Depot increased revenues from $45.7 billion in 2000 to $81.5 billion by 2005, and profits rose from $2.6 billion to $5.8 billion. But customer satisfaction started to slip. Between 2001 and 2005, Home Depot's customer satisfaction fell 11 percent . That's a big drop in itself, but when competition improves, it is even more worrisome. Rival Lowe's customer satisfaction went up by 4 percent. The two retailers had been even in the ACSI in 2001, but four years later, there was a large gap between Lowe's and Home Depot. Now Wall Street did take notice. By early 2006, the five-year stock returns for Home Depot were negative; for Lowe's, the stock price was up by 130 percent. Home Depot had devalued its most critical asset: the health of customer relationships. Culture change had become more like culture shock. While the organization may perhaps have been too loose, it was now rigid and top-down. With fewer frontline staff and more part-timers, there were fewer knowledgeable staff on hand to serve customers. It became difficult to find somebody to help you at Home Depot. The second half of the retailer's slogan—"You can do it. We can help."—turned into a sarcastic joke. Employees took to calling the company "Home Despot," and, in the fourth quarter of 2006, earnings declined by 28 percent with same-store sales down 6.6 percent—the first decline ever for Home Depot. Balance had to be restored. Nardelli was probably trying to change. But it was now too late. He was fired in the beginning of 2007. A few months earlier, however, in the summer of 2006, Home Depot had actually began trying to fix its customer service, investing $350 million in additional human resources to address the problem of not enough frontline staff on the floor and in store improvements such as radio-equipped call boxes strategically placed throughout the store for customers to call for assistance. Management also took steps to improve employee satisfaction, rolling out an incentive program with cash rewards to outstanding employees and stores with exemplary customer service. The effects registered in the ACSI: Customer satisfaction improved by 5 percent, still falling short of Lowe's but a step in the right direction.

AMAZON FIGHTS WALL STREET AND WINS

It takes a strong will and strong company to stand up to the short-term pressures of the stock market. Almost since its inception, Amazon has been a satisfaction leader, not only among e-commerce companies, but also when compared to companies across the economic spectrum. That Amazon has been able to do this consistently is no small feat. But, its efforts have not always been appreciated by investors. One can probably make the argument that Amazon has been wrongfully punished by the stock market because of the inability of accounting to match current cost to future income when assets are intangible. The company has consistently invested in customer service improvements. Even though the benefits of these investments occur in the future, much of their costs are expensed immediately As a result, the recorded short-term earnings are probably lower than the actual earnings.

When Amazon first opened its "virtual" doors in 1994, the company was on the cutting edge of the e-commerce revolution as one of the first in the world to offer goods over the Internet. Focused exclusively on book sales, Amazon founder Jeff Bezos saw e-commerce's potential to offer a far wider range of book titles than was possible in the traditional brick-and-mortar bookstore. His business model inspired the company's name change to Amazon, in reference to the world's most voluminous river. What Bezos set out to achieve was a channel that offered customers a broader, much more "voluminous" selection of books than any other bookseller.

Amazon was an almost instant success. After only a few months in business, sales were in the tens of thousands of dollars each week. Bezos considered customer experience-enhancing improvements to the website as important priorities. He was first with "one-click" shopping, customer reviews, and purchase verification over e-mail. The company went public in 1997, and by 1998, Amazon began pursuing additional revenue streams: music, videos, and toys, among many other things. But unlike many of the dot-coms during this period, Amazon followed a strategy that deliberately delayed (accounting) profits in exchange for longer-term and more sustainable revenue growth. In fact, Bezos didn't expect to generate profits for several years—and said as much. While investors complained about lack of profitability, Amazon's management was insistent on reinvesting capital, aimed to some extent at new customer and business acquisition, but also at providing service enhancements and technological innovations that would better guarantee strong customer relationships based on customer satisfaction.

Amazon has continued to add to its product portfolio. While not as expansive as e-commerce competitor eBay, the Amazon portfolio allows customers to purchase tools, jewelry, electronics, gourmet food, office supplies, and clothes in addition to books. Customer satisfaction has remained strong. This is quite remarkable. I thought that it would drop. After all, books are a fairly simple product. Consumers know how to use them. Books don't need much service. Short of getting the wrong book, getting it late, or not receiving it at all, customer service is not a major challenge. But this cannot be said for Amazon's new product portfolio. Tools require instructions; jewelry can be the wrong size or damaged; electronics are difficult to program and operate; food goes bad, etc. Yet, through it all, Amazon has maintained very high levels of customer satisfaction. Not only is this difficult to do, but it is even more difficult to do in the face of investor criticism. True, the company didn't record a profit until the fourth quarter of 2002. And even though Amazon has been profitable every year since, it has often been accused of not generating enough wealth for shareholders. In early 2007, Amazon reported profits of $190 million on almost $11 billion in revenues, a margin of 1.8 percent. One Goldman Sachs analyst summed up the Wall Street sentiment on Amazon and its profitability when, speaking to the *Wall Street Journal*, he said, "the company [Amazon] continues to disappoint in profitability, so it's hard to give credit for revenue growth."[6] And sure enough, shortly after the earnings release, the stock slumped. As a matter of fact, this reaction is now pretty predictable. In early February of each year, disappointing quarterly and year-end profit statements lead to a drop in market value, with investors punishing the company for its below-expectations performance. But this seems to be a short-term, almost knee-jerk reaction that is corrected later on. I bought Amazon shares just after such a reaction. Six months later, in early June 2007, my return on those shares was 80 percent.

Table 4.1 Amazon's Punishment—Adjusted Closing Price day of and day after 4th Quarter/Year-End Financial Statement Releases

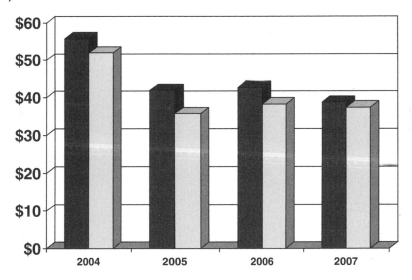

I am not sure what Amazon has that makes it withstand the short-term pressures of Wall Street—something Circuit City has been unable to muster—but the fact of the matter is that Amazon has kept its focus on customers at the expense of short-term profitability.

I am sure customers appreciate this. Shareholders should too. In 2006, for example, Amazon added many new products and services, new partnerships to distribute for other companies, and, most importantly, dozens of system upgrades for better customer service. Just for the fourth quarter of 2006, Amazon's spending on technology and content increased 34 percent to $177 million. This expenditure involves mostly hiring new staff (i.e., web developers and computer scientists) to work on improving existing infrastructure and web systems—only a limited percentage of such outlays can be capitalized, and they therefore don't appear on the balance sheet. Nevertheless, there will come a time when investments in customer satisfaction must pay a dividend in earnings. In other words, short-term profits may not matter, but there have to be long-term profits. Stock price will not rise if Amazon's customer service outlays continue in perpetuity. If that's the case, then the business model would have to be called into question.

CHAPTER 5

Customer Satisfaction and Stock Returns: The Power of the Obvious

THE POWER OF THE OBVIOUS

We have a new coffee machine in the faculty lounge. When I moved to the United States some 30 years ago, coffee was a different drink than it is today. Now, there are many kinds of coffee available and one can even get good espresso from a coffee machine. Today I was up earlier than usual, preparing for media interviews scheduled for the afternoon. In the far-end corner of the lounge, sitting in an easy chair, was Paul McCracken, head sticking up above the newspaper he was reading. Paul had joined the Michigan faculty in 1948, and, as far as I knew, was the only one who was still around from those days. Some 20 years after he joined the Michigan faculty, he became chairman of President Nixon's Council of Economic Advisers. Now almost another 40 years later, Paul was emeritus professor and I would bump into him in the halls of the business school every now and then. He had been an early patron of the ACSI and was one of those individuals who could compact a web of interconnected ideas into a single sentence of a few words.

"Paul," I said, "Take a look at this," as I showed him a graph of ACSI and stock returns. "Companies with highly satisfied customers do much better in the stock market than others. They always beat the market."

I waited for his response. It was true that investments in customer satisfaction, by corporations and investors, led to excess returns and I had the data to prove it. Would Paul ask if these returns were associated with higher risk? I knew the answer to that question. We might even have stumbled upon the Holy Grail—for managers as well as investors: Satisfied customers are economic assets with *high* returns and *low* risks. That is, you don't have to take high risks in order to get high returns. This is contrary to what most financial analysts believe. It is also contrary to what many in business believe: "Be bold—take risks. No risk, no reward. Nothing ventured, nothing gained."

But risk can be trimmed and it can be reduced. That's what knowledge is for: removing or reducing uncertainty. People in the know assume less risk than the rest of us. And they usually win. But in finance and in business, the notion of high risk/high return is so ingrained that *low* risk/high return seems either implausible or puzzling. Paul didn't think long. "Well," he said with a smile. "If that wasn't so, we'd have to go back to the drawing board about how the economy works."

Was it really that obvious? If the satisfaction of a company's customers didn't have anything to do with its stock price, there was something wrong with our understanding of how capitalistic market theory works. Walking back to my office, I concluded that Paul was right. In retrospect, it *was* obvious. All we had done was to confirm a basic principle of how product markets and equity markets exercise joint power. But why didn't more people see this? How was it possible to beat the market year after year by investing in firms with strong customer relationships?

The research literature presented a good deal of evidence behind the fact that there was a relationship between customer satisfaction and economic returns in general,[1] but not much was known about how the satisfaction of companies' customers translates into securities pricing, and virtually nothing was known about the associated risks. Yet, the link between buyer utility and the allocation of investment capital is a fundamental principle upon which the economic system of free market capitalism obviously rests. The degree to which capital flows from investors actually do move in tandem with customer satisfaction is a matter of considerable importance because it is an indication of how well (or poorly) markets actually function. In a monopoly, for example, dissatisfied buyers cannot punish the seller by taking their business elsewhere. Therefore, capital flows would not correspond to consumer utility. But, according to theory, that would impede the efficiency of resource allocation in the economy. Efficient allocation of resources and consumer sovereignty depend on the ability of both product and capital markets to reward and to punish. Those failing to satisfy their customers would be doubly punished—by both customer defection and capital withdrawal. Similarly, sellers doing well by their customers would be doubly rewarded—by more business from customers and more capital from investors. So far, so good. This is straightforward.

WHAT DETERMINES STOCK PRICE?

I was trying to estimate the relationship between customer satisfaction and market value of equity. As I had expected, we found a strong relationship no matter how we specified our equations. That prompted an examination of how investors react to ACSI news about changes in customer satisfaction. There was no evidence that they reacted in a timely manner. Was that because they knew already and the satisfaction news was somehow factored into share prices, or was there some other explanation? I knew that reality was not necessarily the same as theory here. And even though both neoclassical economic theory and textbook marketing principles suggested a positive relationship between customer satisfaction and stock prices, I had seen many exceptions to that rule. In fact, I could think of circumstances in which the relationship would be negative.

In talks to industry groups and to investors, I make the point that quality matters more than generally thought and that economic growth depends on the productivity of economic resources *and* the quality of the output (as experienced by the user) that those resources generate. Expanding economic activity per se is not what's most essential. Economic theory considers consumer utility, or satisfaction, to be the real standard for economic growth. The extent to which buyers financially reward sellers that satisfy them and punish those who don't, and the degree to which investment capital reinforces the power of the consumer, is what matters. Capitalistic free markets are built on the idea that for a market to function well, it must allocate resources in order to create the greatest possible consumer satisfaction as efficiently as possible. On this point, common sense and economic theory converge: A dissatisfied buyer will not return to the same seller unless there is nowhere else to go, or it is too expensive to make a change. Limitations on consumer sovereignty might be helpful to the monopolist, but not to the economy at large. In a competitive market, firms that do well by their customers are rewarded by repeat business, lower price elasticity, higher reservation prices, more cross-selling opportunities, greater marketing efficiency, and a host of other things that usually lead to earnings growth.[2]

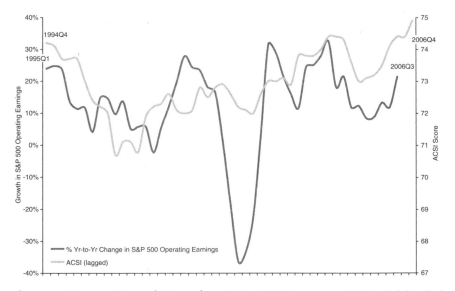

Figure 5.1 ACSI and Growth in S&P 500 Earnings: 1995–2006 Q4

Source: S & P 500 Operating Earnings from Standards and Poor at spglobal.com

Figure 5.1 shows that corporate earnings are aligned with customer satisfaction; in most businesses, companies do compete for the satisfaction of their customers. If they succeed, it is reflected in their earnings. One would think it would be reflected in stock prices and company valuations as well.

There is no mystery as to what causes a company's market value to rise: (1) acceleration of cash flows; (2) increase in cash flows; (3) reduction of risk associated with cash flows; and (4) increase in the residual value of the business. This is well documented in an article by Rajendra Srivastava and his colleagues.[3] Not only does the customer asset as defined by the expected future discounted net cash flow from current and future customers affect all four of these, but it is really the sum of all other economic assets.

Because the necessary selling effort, by implication, is less when dealing with a satisfied customer and because it's more likely that receivable turnover is quicker for firms with satisfied customers, speed of cash flow is positively affected: Marginal costs of sales and marketing are lower. The same is true for working capital and fixed investment. At the same time, revenue benefits from more repeat business. We also know that an increase in customer satisfaction contributes both to cash flow growth and to less variability in cash flows. As a result, cost of capital goes down and we have another source for stock price growth.

INVESTOR REACTION

Almost no matter how we analyzed the data or which time periods we looked at, we always got a strong and significant relationship between customer satisfaction and market value of equity and between customer satisfaction and earnings. On the average, the "equity elasticity" was 4.6 percent, which means that a 1 percent improvement in customer satisfaction relates to a 4.6 percent increase in market value. This is a big number, but I caution against exaggerated interpretations. It's an average and the research model upon which it is based has limited cause-and-effect properties. But it is big and it is significant.

But we also found something else. The higher the level of customer satisfaction, the less a company's liabilities lessen market value. In other words, a firm with high levels of customer satisfaction is able to take on more debt than a firm with less satisfied customers, without adversely affecting share price.

Our next task was to examine how investors react to news about customer satisfaction. Do they take advantage of the fact that customer satisfaction is a leading indicator of financial performance or is the information already factored into share prices? Do investors reward firms with more capital, as news about the improved value of customer relationships becomes available? How about bad news? In fact, I already knew that there might be circumstances under which stock prices would actually fall when customer satisfaction increased. True, this would be at odds with how capitalistic markets should function, but it may happen because of market imperfections. For example, investors may react negatively to news about rising customer satisfaction if they thought that the firm was giving away too much to the buyers. The difference between the maximum price a buyer might be willing to pay and the actual price is something that investors may want to get their hands on. Why give it to the customers? If the customers' cost of going elsewhere is high or if there are restrictions on consumer choice, investors would be reluctant to give up too much. Try to get out of a cell-phone contract early. That's going to cost you. According to the *New York Times*,[4] most mobile phone companies will wave termination fees only if you die, but they will make sure that you are dead by asking for a death certificate. Under such circumstances, it's less likely that customer satisfaction and stock prices move together.

Investors might also not care much for improvements in customer satisfaction for firms that already are way above their competition in customer satisfaction, because the marginal return for improving customer satisfaction further may then be too small. For services that are labor intensive, it is also uncertain if the additional satisfaction of the customer will offset the increasing cost of labor. Another complicating factor is "reverse causality." Customer defection has a positive effect on average customer satisfaction because the departing customers were the most dissatisfied to begin with. Those remaining are less discontented. What's happening is that the company retains a shrinking group of more satisfied customers. This has happened to Jaguar cars and to many newspapers: Both revenues and profits fall. Stock prices, too. But not average customer satisfaction. It goes up, but for the wrong reason.

It is also difficult to get a good idea of what the stock market-expectations about customer satisfaction might be. I have no idea how to gauge such expectations, but they may have large short-term effects. In the long term, they matter much less.

And, sure enough, we could not detect any systematic reaction in the stock market as a result of news about customer satisfaction. We compared stock prices before and after information from the ACSI was released. I also set up a stock portfolio in which 50 percent of the trades were done before the release and 50 percent after the release. There was no difference in returns.

WHY DON'T PROFESSIONAL STOCK PICKERS DO A BETTER JOB?

Even though news about customer satisfaction does not move stock prices, it's still possible that stock markets are efficient. If they are, then share prices would reflect all relevant information all the time and it would be a fluke if somebody time and again could beat the market. But just because there wasn't any investor reaction to news about customer satisfaction doesn't mean that stock markets are inefficient. Nor does it mean that it's not possible for firms with highly satisfied customers to generate higher profits. It wouldn't be possible, however, to consistently beat the stock market if the market was efficient. Indeed, it is difficult to find anybody who has. At least because of skill. Luck is a different matter. The probability of finding a four-leaf clover is very low, but the probability that there is at least one four-leaf clover in any sizeable grassy field is very high. Out of more than 10,000 stock traders in the United States, luck alone suggests that about 5,000 of them should beat the market in any given year. The probability is high that a few of them will do it year after year. But the probability of finding such a trader before the fact is harder than finding a four-leaf clover. Of course, it would be equally difficult for someone to do worse than the market. Even if one tried hard to make the most stupid investments imaginable, it wouldn't be possible to completely defy the laws of probability.

But I don't know if stock markets are efficient or not. What I do know is that they are either not efficient or less than perfectly efficient. If they were perfectly efficient, only inside traders—or people with a rabbit's foot—would have excess returns. It would also be difficult to explain why random chance has a long string of victories over professional investment managers and brokerage firms. Actively managed funds rarely outperform index funds.[5] According to Ken Fisher, the CEO of Fisher Investments, a highly successful money management firm with $30 billion in assets, there is really only one thing that matters: the extent to which you know something that others don't.[6] He, too, points out that few professionals consistently beat the market.

When I was looking at our early statistics on the relationship between the ACSI and stock prices, I was surprised by just how poor the record of the professionals was. Between 1997 and 2001, the market gained more than 70 percent, but many brokerage houses had negative results. Those who followed Fleet Boston Financial's stock advice lost 36 percent[7]—more than 100 percent worse than one would have done by picking stocks at random. Even the best recommendations, those given by Credit Suisse First Boston, delivered a meager 7.6 percent. Dart throwing would have done better.

What about mutual funds? Those that beat the market in the past were almost never able to keep on doing it.[8] How about hedge funds? Surely, they must be doing better. After all, they charge their investors much higher fees than mutual funds. And they have attracted more than $1 trillion in capital in the United States alone. But they perform no better than mutual funds and also fail to beat the market.[9] Why aren't the professionals doing better? A major thesis of this book is that knowledge matters. Professionals ought to have that knowledge. Otherwise, they shouldn't be called professionals. But is there something else at work here? If professionals *consistently* lose to random chance, markets cannot be efficient. If they consistently win, markets can't be efficient either. Markets might be unpredictable, according to Robert Shiller of Yale University. But just because they are unpredictable doesn't mean that they are inefficient.[10] A good amount has been written about conflicts of interest when stock analysts work for investment bankers, but there is not sufficient evidence to explain why analysts in general would regularly bet on losers. If they look to buy low and sell high, but end up doing the converse, perhaps the information they use is systematically distorted. As I have alluded to earlier, there's no shortage of information distortion here. Accounting (this goes for both corporate and national accounting) records assets of dwindling relevance to the modern economy about companies' future financial prospects. The disconnect between the historical costs of assets, which is what gets recorded on the balance sheet, and their market value keeps growing.

Ken Fisher has a point. If you know something that others don't, chances are that you'll do better. Do customers know something that investors don't? To Paul McCracken, it seems obvious that they do. And he is right. They do and it is obvious. I didn't realize this when I was in the middle of trying to figure out the effects of customer satisfaction. But I was not alone. Most of us don't realize the obvious until it is pointed out by somebody else. The Securities and Exchange Commission (SEC) didn't see it either.

The *Wall Street Journal* wrote an article about my stock portfolio returns and wondered whether my returns were related to insider trading. I knew that my returns had nothing to do with insider trading, but they did come from knowing something that others couldn't figure out. I had a technology for extracting forward-looking information from a customer aggregate and a theory for how to pick stocks accordingly. Since there was no effect on share prices from the release of the ACSI scores, the timing of the ACSI release had nothing to do with it. But context does. The buy-and-sell signals from customer satisfaction information cannot be interpreted without context. The SEC looked into it and found no evidence of insider trading. The *Wall Street Journal*, to its credit, wrote another article (although not on the front page this time) about my "good run in the market and with regulators."[11] The "good run" has since continued and I expect it to do so in the future as well. As long as repeat business is important and buyers have choice, customer satisfaction will be a most relevant factor in the prediction of a company's capacity to generate returns for its shareholders.

PLAY MONEY

My first test about the relevance of customer satisfaction in stock trading was with a hypothetical paper portfolio with simple trading rules, not with real money. Because investors didn't react to changes in the ACSI, it seemed reasonable to base the strategy both on levels of customer satisfaction (since they didn't appear to be fully impounded in the stock prices) and changes in customer satisfaction (since they didn't appear to be at all reflected in stock prices). In order to have a diversified portfolio of practical size, firms in the top 20 percent of the ACSI, relative to their competition, were selected. Since I knew that too low a level of customer satisfaction often didn't have much of an impact, the selection was also made conditional on the requirement of being above the ACSI national average.

Shares were "purchased" the day the ACSI results were announced and held for a year or longer. If a stock was picked the first year, its inclusion in the portfolio was examined again the following year. If it met the criteria of being in the top 20 percent and above the national (average) ACSI level, it was held for another year and then subjected to the same test. If it failed the criteria, it was sold. The same principle was applied for all stocks. If a stock was not picked the first year, it was re-examined for inclusion the next year and so on. This trading strategy led to a portfolio of 20 companies in 1997, 20 in 1998, ending up with 26 companies at the conclusion of the test on May 21, 2003. We reported the results in the January 2006 issue of the *Journal of Marketing*.[12] A curious choice of outlet, perhaps, but the theory we developed has very little to do with traditional stock picking or finance, and a great deal to do with marketing theory.

Between February 18, 1997, and May 21, 2003, a time period when the stock market had both ups and downs, the portfolio generated a cumulative return of 40 percent. It outperformed the Dow Jones Industrials by 93 percent, the S&P 500 by 201 percent, and NAS-DAQ by 335 percent.

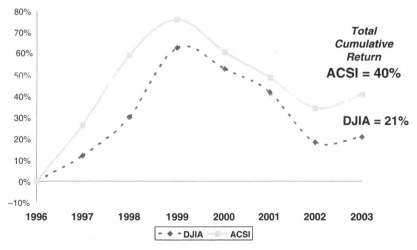

Figure 5.2 Cumulative Returns: A Simple Back Test ACSI vs. DJIA, 1997–2003*

* 2/18/1997 to 5/21/2003

It seemed that we had it right. Investments in customer satisfaction pay off in up-markets as well as in down-markets. What we found is very important for business managers as well as stock investors. The manager can be more confident that investments into better customer relationships will pay off—showing up in higher market valuation for the company. The investor would be well advised to pay attention to the relevance of changes in customer assets. When the stock market grew, the stock prices of many firms with highly satisfied customers grew even more. The only exception occurred at the peak of the stock market bubble in 1999, when NASDAQ and the S&P 500 generated short-lived, but higher, returns. When the stock market dropped in value, the stock prices of firms with highly satisfied customers were better protected.

Could there be other explanations for our results? This was the question I got from presenting the research in business meetings and academic seminars in Spain, Italy, France, Sweden, China, England, Denmark, and the United States. Let's see. My first argument was that it is difficult to beat the market. I didn't mean this in a literal sense, because it isn't that hard to beat the market if you have (relevant) knowledge that others don't have. But it was a good starting point. Most people seemed to agree. But, there is always the possibility that I was just lucky. But luck has no explanation. It's random. And I had an explanation. I could explain the results. And I could do it with conventional economics and marketing theory. I could also talk in probability terms. Under virtually all assumptions, the probability that the returns were due to luck was exceedingly low. Disposing with luck and turning to economics as an explanation, one could simply point out that sellers are supposed to compete for the satisfaction of their customers. Efficient allocation of resources in the economy depends on the joint ability of product and capital markets to reward and punish companies. In reality, it depends on how much choice the consumer really has and how easy it might be to "punish" a faltering supplier or to reward a good one.

Another question I would get had to do with risk. Paul McCracken didn't ask me this, but almost every financial economist did. Perhaps I was getting these results as a compensation for taking higher risk, they suggested. I understood the question, and the answer was obvious. At least, it was to me. Having satisfied customers reduces business risk. The customer base is then more dependable and less volatile. Satisfied customers are the most reluctant to leave and the most likely to buy more. It doesn't mean that they won't leave if presented with an alternative, but it must be an attractive one. We looked into a number of other possible explanations, such as firm size and price-to-earnings ratios, which might possibly explain our findings, but none of them did.

THE HOLY GRAIL?

Had we found the Holy Grail here? Low risk and high return? For investors, maybe. For managers, there is another piece of uncertainty—the skill with which customer satisfaction improvements are implemented—to deal with. But let's recall the importance of knowledge, context, and prediction. Prediction is less difficult if you have knowledge and understand the context within which it can be applied. The future is far from random. If you know things that others don't, chances are that you predict better too.

Note that we didn't get these returns from technical analysis of share price patterns. We are a bit closer to fundamental analysis, which is about determining the future value of cash flows, but otherwise, this has little to do with finance or investment practice. We had no help from accounting either. We're looking at the source of (non-financial) revenue and cost, which is customers. If we understand the source of cash, we can better predict its flow. And we get an extra boost from the fact that the balance of power between buyers and sellers is shifting in favor of buyers. The more we know about those who have power, the better off we'll be. True in general, true in business and stock picking. Not only did we beat the market, but we killed the professionals: Most brokerage firms had *negative* abnormal returns over this period of time.[13]

BUT IT'S ONLY A GAME

But, before getting overly excited, let's remember that we are only playing a game. There is no money on the table. So far, our research only involves play money and back testing. Can we replicate the results using real money? As with all back testing of stock portfolios, there are major limitations. Perhaps we were so eager to find good results that we somehow tricked ourselves into finding them? In hindsight, it may not be all that difficult to find a successful stock trading strategy. All you have to do is rearrange the data until you find some nice results. I don't think we did that, but there's always a risk that you might find what you're looking for if there is very little cost associated with the search and there are many "good" solutions. In this sense, it was actually encouraging that all our stock picks had not been good ones. Gateway Computers was a terrible choice and a lot of (play) money was lost. It was purchased on August 21, 2000, because it had an ACSI score of 78 (which was in the top 20 percent of its industry and above the national average). It was sold, as it dropped out of the top 20 percent, on August 20, 2001. Over that period of time, its stock price fell by 84 percent. What happened was that (1) overall consumer demand for personal computers fell sharply and (2) Dell crushed Gateway. Later, we did pick up on Dell's subsequent decline well ahead of time.

No stock trading strategy will work for every company all the time. There are other factors at play and there is a random component as well: if the future has more randomness and/or there are factors, unknown to us, affecting it. Either way, our forecast is not going to be very good. There is also little reason to believe that high customer satisfaction can provide full stock market insulation if consumer demand for an entire industry falters. It should dampen the fall to some degree, but that's about all. However, if we have a diversified portfolio, adverse industry effects would be offset by positive ones. Here is where Dell comes in. It produced a return of 50 percent during a one-year period. And, of course, there were other stocks that more than made up for the losses on Gateway. Otherwise, we wouldn't have the returns we got.

REAL MONEY, REAL RETURNS

I was confident that we had it right. I knew it before we had completed the back testing. We had theory. We had data. Both pointed in the same direction. I was prepared to put my own money on the line and create a real stock portfolio of ACSI companies. I also thought I could improve on the returns by taking both long and short positions. I'd go long in companies with strong customer satisfaction and short in companies with weak customer satisfaction. But, this was still a test. As with the play money portfolio, it would be useful to see how the strategy worked in both up-markets and down-markets.

I got my wish regarding down-markets first. A bit more than I wanted to. Trading started in April 2000—just before the stock bubble burst. I lost money that year. The value of the portfolio dropped by almost 10 percent by the end of the year. But the market did even worse. The S&P 500 went down by 12 percent. Still, this was not much to brag about. But eight months were not enough for drawing conclusions. The market continued to fall in 2001. It dropped another 13 percent.

But I was celebrating. The customer satisfaction portfolio was up by 10 percent. This was a big win. After no more than a year and a half, the portfolio was doing much better than the market. Would this continue? Yes, but the market took a whopping in 2002. It fell by

147

another 23 percent. How could companies, even with the most satisfied customers, withstand this? They did, but not totally. The portfolio value fell by 6 percent. Not bad, though.

During three consecutive years of large losses for the stock market, the ACSI portfolio had outperformed the market by a wide margin and for each and every year, it had done better than market. Apparently, having very satisfied customers does protect you in a down-market. What about up-markets? Would the theory still hold? Could we make more money than an index fund? The first check came in 2003. The stock market rebounded from three years of heavy losses. The S&P 500 gained 26 percent. But the customer satisfaction portfolio did better. It went up by 36 percent.

That was it. Enough evidence. With the help of Sunil, Forrest, and Krishnan, I wrote up the results in a paper and submitted it for review in the *Journal of Marketing.* The reviews came back asking for clarification of returns and more on the theoretical underpinnings. The reviewers agreed that the results were quite extraordinary but wanted to make sure that they were obtained from correct analysis. They also wanted more explanation and a thorough analysis of possible explanations other than customer satisfaction. Were there any other explanations? We looked at a number of possibilities as suggested by the comments from reviewers, but they were all eliminated. We could find no explanation other than customer satisfaction. I am sure that other researchers will look closely for other possible explanations and maybe there are factors that are highly related to customer satisfaction that play a role. But, from a practical perspective, I am not sure it matters. We were making a lot of money.

All reviewers agreed that we had done the analysis of investor reaction to ACSI news correctly: There was no investor reaction. One reviewer then concluded that because investors did not react, we could not reject the null hypothesis and therefore the paper was of limited value. But the rejection of the hypothesis that investors reacted was key. In statistical testing terminology, the null hypothesis implied that investors didn't react to news about customer satisfaction. A rejection of that hypothesis would have made our paper of much less interest, because we would then only have verified what was known already and it wouldn't have been possible to come up with a stock portfolio that outperformed the market. We also clarified that our results didn't depend on financial theory. They obviously didn't depend on efficient markets. We were also asked to collect stock price data on all firms in the ACSI that we didn't invest in. The performance of those firms turned out to be nearly identical to the market.

After having made the appropriate changes, the paper was accepted for publication. But we had one additional year of results by then and these results were included in the final manuscript. The up-market continued in 2004. And again, the customer satisfaction portfolio performed as we had predicted. The market went up by 9 percent, handily beaten by our portfolio, which had a 32 percent increase.

But the real test comes after you have had a good run and published your results. Here is where most stock pickers fail. It is easy enough to find somebody who has done well in the past, but they rarely continue to do well.[14] We had shown that a portfolio based on customer satisfaction outperformed the S&P 500 in both up-markets and down-markets And this occurred every year. We had three consecutive down-markets and two consecutive up-markets. Our cumulative return was 75 percent; the corresponding S&P 500 return was -19 percent. Would these results hold up in the future? What happened in 2005, 2006, and 2007? The stock market continued to do well. And the customer satisfaction portfolio went up even more. In 2005, the market gained 8 percent; our portfolio gained 16 percent. In 2006, it was a bit closer. The portfolio gained 16 percent—the same as in 2005 and the market was up by 14 percent. By the end of May 2007, the market was up by 8 percent. The

ACSI portfolio was at 15 percent with an annualized three-year return of 24 percent.

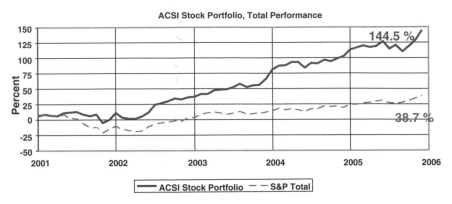

Figure 5.3 CSat Fund Five-Year Performance

The cumulative five-year returns were strong as well. Between 2001 and 2006, the ACSI fund returned 145 percent, compared with 39 percent for the S&P 500 total (including dividends). I am not aware of any mutual fund or stock portfolio in this class, large-cap U.S. consumer goods, that has had better returns.

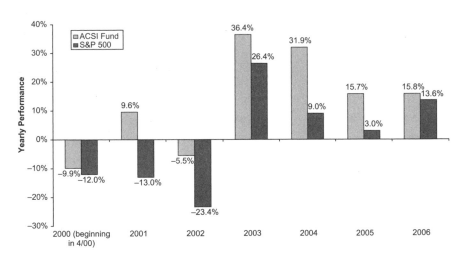

Figure 5.4 Yearly Performance of ACSI Fund and S&P 500: April 2000 (Inception)–December 2006 (TWR Return)

As with the play money portfolio, the returns were not due to high risk. The systematic risk, the correlation to market, was about the same. But in looking at the correlation to market over time, I also found that it was a lot lower in down-markets than it was in up-markets. In down-markets, it was 74 percent. In up-markets, it was 115 percent. That meant that the portfolio didn't follow the market all that much when it was going down. In up-markets, it did. That's another nice feature. If we invest in satisfied customers, our share price is not dragged down when the market drops, and it goes up proportionally more when the market goes up.

The short positions did not do as well as the long. Betting against a firm with weak customer satisfaction didn't work quite as well. But I am not ready to conclude that the market rewards high customer satisfaction more than it punishes dissatisfaction. Consumers are getting more empowered. If they haven't already, they will exercise that power more in the future. Just remember what happened to Dell, Ford, Charter Communications, Circuit City, or Qwest Communications.

By any standard, the portfolio returns are quite exceptional. Not only do they show that investments, based on information about the satisfaction of customers, produce sizeable excess returns, but they also upset the basic financial principle that assets producing high returns must also have high risk. According to fundamental analysis, the price of a financial asset is determined by the current value of the future cash payments it generates, discounted to compensate for risk and cost of capital. Firms that do better than their competition in terms of satisfying customers generate superior returns at lower systematic risk. According to Gupta, Lehmann, and Stuart (2004),[15] financial analysts have yet to give more than scant attention to off-balance-sheet assets even though these assets may be key determinants of a firm's market value. By employing a discounted cash flow analysis for estimating the value of customer relationships, they found that some companies were potentially mispriced while others were not. In general though, our results suggest that companies with strong customer satisfaction may remain under-priced, but only for a while. This might change in the future. For now, however, it does seem to take some time for stock markets to reward firms that do well by their customers and punish those that don't. For business managers, it is clear that the cost of managing customer relationships and the cash flows they produce are fundamental to value creation and subsequent share price movement, but the rewards are not instant. Not yet anyway.

Even though customer satisfaction is strongly related to share prices and the (collective) customer may have information relevant to the financial prospects of the firm before investors do, these facts cannot be leveraged if the customer satisfaction measurement is flawed and therefore unable to extract the information. Unfortunately, the current state of affairs is not good. Too many companies have too primitive systems for customer satisfaction measurement. A few years ago, David Larcker of Stanford University and Chris Ittner at the Wharton School did a systematic inventory of current practice and found measurement technology to be seriously wanting. They concluded that most were "mindless," misleading, and too primitive" to be useful.[16] This is consistent with my own experience. For some reason, measurement technology seems to be the worst in information-technology firms. I don't know why this is, but even the most elementary issues are often not attended to.

As far as investors are concerned, they are slow to react but eventually get it right. It may be slow and it may be indirect, but there is a relationship between consumer utility and the flow of investment capital. Even though it takes a while for equity markets and consumer markets to exercise their joint power, the finding that customer satisfaction and stock prices eventually move together is reassuring. It suggests that most markets work well in the long run. Short-term fluctuations and other exceptions notwithstanding, managers should take comfort in the fact that they usually, albeit not immediately, get rewarded for treating customers well or risk punishment for treating them badly. Chances are that both rewards and punishments will magnify in the future. The speed at which they will be exercised will no doubt increase.

CHAPTER 6

Things Aren't Always What They Seem: Inadvertently Damaging Customer Assets

Though I may not know the inner workings of my Dell computer, the problem was obvious to even a moderately computer-literate user: My writable CD-ROM drive was not working—at all. It had been faulty from day one, and finally it quit altogether. Jeff Duncan, my company's go-to guy for all things related to computing systems, took a look. "You'll have to call Dell and get it replaced," he told me. After rummaging through a box of old receipts and warranties, I found the paperwork with the 1–800 number for Dell's customer service line. I had paid the extra cost of an in-home repair contract, so this should be easy, I thought. I placed the call and was routed to an automated menu. After spending two or three minutes listening to menu options followed by more menu options, I arrived at the relevant choice options. After another few minutes of waiting, time spent listening to a few hit tunes from the 1970s, I was greeted by a person on the other end of the line asking what my problem was and how she could help. All in all, not bad.

But soon it become clear that we were not getting anywhere, going back and forth over the problem, me trying to explain the situation, the technician trying to decipher my non-technical description. I had thought this was a simple enough: I had a defective part and it needed to be repaired or replaced. I had paid for somebody to come to my house and solve the problem. Why were we having this prolonged conversation at all? What I didn't know was that Dell apparently tries to solve the problem first over the phone for an hour before the customer is allowed to set up an appointment for home repair. In fact, this is what I was told after about 15 minutes of nonsense conversation. The call center service person and I played a waiting game, watching the clock. I was put on hold a few times. In the end, I got an appointment scheduled (and, as it turned out, the CD-ROM drive had to be replaced, as I knew from the start), but this service encounter was not a productive one—a waste of my time, the call center's time, and Dell's time. It didn't make for a satisfied customer, either. I am sure this is not what Michael Dell had in mind, but these are the kinds of things that may well happen as we try to balance service effort and cutting cost. This is why customer service experiences like this are not uncommon.

Balancing cost and quality is central to any business. Dell got it wrong by placing too much weight on attention to certain types of costs to the detriment of its customer relationships. But Dell is not unique. It has become very common, as a way to control the cost of labor-intensive functions, to outsource customer service to areas with lower labor costs. Our research has shown that when offshoring is done for back office functions such as IT, customer satisfaction can actually improve. But often it's the front office functions that are offshored. That's when customer satisfaction usually suffers. The problem is that the actual—but unrecorded—costs as a result of deteriorating customer relationships. This is especially relevant with offshore call centers. One of CFI Group's partners did a study about American customers' satisfaction with domestic versus offshore call centers and found that the difference in satisfaction was huge. The average user satisfaction with call centers based in the United States was more than 60 percent higher than the average satisfaction with offshore call centers. The problem was particularly acute for companies like Dell when people called to get help with technical problems.

"You've got people trying to answer technical questions in a language that's not necessarily their first language," said Sheri Teodoru, the CFI partner responsible for the study. "How do you translate 'doohickey'? It's just a recipe for miscommunication."[1]

But it doesn't have to be this way. If quality of service is better balanced against cost efficiencies, we can do much better. In fairness to Dell, its founder has acknowledged this as well: "We were doing some things that were just plain wrong . . . The team was managing cost instead of service and quality."[2]

So, how do we get things right? Counterexamples might be useful. A good starting point might be to look at what to avoid. Once the most common mistakes have been identified, we'll be in a better position to do things right. Let's discuss mistakes, expose myths, and clarify misunderstandings. And let's address some of the most common questions along the way: Should we strive to maximize customer satisfaction? Does it make sense to try to exceed our customers' expectations? How do we treat complaints? Does lowering price lead to higher customer satisfaction? What effect do mergers and acquisitions have on the value of customer assets? Let me begin with perhaps the most misunderstood of all: customer complaints.

MAXIMIZE CUSTOMER COMPLAINTS, NOT CUSTOMER SATISFACTION

It may sound contradictory to all logic. My doctoral advisor gave me a funny look when, many years ago back in Sweden, I told him about my findings. I had done the math. I had set up the right equations. I had taken the partial derivatives of just about everything. The answer was clear. Profit maximizing firms should strive to maximize customer complaints. "Is that what they taught you at Berkeley?" he asked.

It wasn't. I knew I was correct, but I had been too deep into the math to come up with a simple explanation. Once I was out of the trees and could see the forest, it became almost derisorily simple: Companies should maximize the number of complaints, relative to the number of dissatisfied customers, because the opportunity costs of not doing so are higher than dealing with the complaint. Simple economics.

Similarly, customer satisfaction shouldn't be maximized—not from the seller's perspective. The marginal cost of maximizing customer satisfaction would exceed the marginal revenue associated with it. The *buyer* is supposed to maximize utility (satisfaction); the *seller* is supposed to maximize profits. The two should not be confused. Even though customer retention can produce increasing rates of return over some retention interval, there will be diminishing returns at some point. At the extreme, we would either give away, or perhaps pay the buyer to take, our products. We might expel customers in order to lavishly serve a few. Neither strategy is likely to be profitable. As Dell learned, of all the frustrations customers experience with call centers, one of the most irritating is waiting time. The usual way to address this issue is to open more lines and hire more service staff to take calls. Spending more money on improving hold time on the phone is fine, but how much money? At what point does the marginal cost exceed the marginal revenue? Whole Foods in New York figured this out by changing from the usual super market system of multiple cashier lines to a single line and more cash registers. As a result, check out time is 50 percent faster than competing chains. The implication: more transactions processed, higher sales, high customer satisfaction, greater profit margins.[3]

How quickly should calls be answered? A couple of years ago, we worked with a food company to determine the point where additional resources and staffing for its call center wouldn't be profitable. As it turned out, the optimal waiting time was 30 seconds, somewhat higher than the company believed its customers would find acceptable. Reducing it further wouldn't have improved customer satisfaction and would have cost the company several million dollars—money that could be better used for other purposes.

What about waiting to get through customs? That is something people gripe about. Shortening that wait time should have a positive impact on satisfaction with the experience. The ACSI data on the U.S. Customs and Immigration Service shows that wait time is by far the worst, and least liked, part of dealing with customs. But it doesn't have much of an impact on traveler satisfaction. Reducing wait time, even astronomically, wouldn't improve satisfaction with the customs service much. So next time you find the wait long coming into the United States, blame CFI Group. According to our estimates, overall traveler satisfaction would not go up enough to justify more resources for the customs and immigration service at U.S. international airports. This is not true for every airport, but in general it would be better to deploy resources on other things.

A firm's economic objective is to maximize the value of its assets. Optimization (not maximization) of customer satisfaction with respect to profitability is the name of the game. This is different from maximizing customer satisfaction. Every firm reaches a point where it's no longer profitable to satisfy every customer desire. The best way to retain customers is to treat them well. But some amount of customer dissatisfaction is almost always inevitable. The only caveat to complaint maximization is that we don't increase complaints by increasing customer dissatisfaction. Rather, we take customer dissatisfaction as a given starting point. That is, assuming some degree of customer dissatisfaction, we want to maximize the opportunity of hearing from these customers.

Many consumer problems are surface symptoms of more basic issues. If a symptom is eliminated, another is likely to appear unless the underlying problem is fixed. Customer dissatisfaction may occur at any stage of the purchase process. Analysis should begin with a definition of the situation: first purchase or re-purchase and post-purchase or pre-purchase. The causes for the dissatisfaction experience, as well as the object of complaint, vary across these situations. For example, a post-purchase product complaint may be caused by inflated expectations from inaccurate information; a re-purchase product complaint may be caused by product deterioration or changing consumer tastes; and a pre-purchase complaint may originate from difficulties with getting information, finding a store, not getting sales assistance, etc.

Since brand-switching and customer defection are more frequent expressions of dissatisfaction than complaining, and because complaint handling and analysis are less costly than a proportional drop in sales, it is in the interest of the firm to facilitate complaint communications. If demand is highly quality elastic, it is better to have customer complaints than customer defections.

The root cause of a complaint is often difficult to detect and sometimes difficult to eliminate. A small but significant number of customers of one of the largest Swedish dairy producers complained about the taste of the company's buttermilk. No change had been made in the buttermilk for years, so why would there be sudden complaints about how it tasted? Following some creative analysis by our Stockholm office, it appeared that most of the complainants had one thing in common: a northern dialect. This was the key to figuring out the cause. Buttermilk in the north is different. It is different because the cows are different. The cows are different because the grass is different. The solution was to ship buttermilk from the north to certain areas in the Stockholm region where many people from the north had come to seek better job opportunities.

Changes in the complaint volume say very little about customer satisfaction. While low complaint levels are often believed to indicate high customer satisfaction, it's even more common to interpret a reduction in complaints as an increase in satisfaction, sometimes to the point of setting objectives for lowering complaint volume. This is a counterproductive and somewhat paradoxical objective. A change in complaint frequency cannot automatically be attributed to a change in customer dissatisfaction. A primary goal ought to be to reduce dissatisfaction (and increase satisfaction), but the complaint is an expression of a grievance with a product or the service accompanying it, or with any element involved in the consumer's shopping or purchase experience. It doesn't necessarily involve the consumer's shopping or purchase experience. It doesn't necessarily involve a product malfunction or a breakdown, nor does it presume that a purchase has been made. Complaints can be about poor service, insufficient breadth or depth of merchandise, long waiting lines, limited parking space, impractical packaging, etc.

Except in cases of sheer frustration or complaining as a last resort, it is not likely that a consumer will complain to a company unless he or she expects the reward to be greater that the effort and perhaps the unpleasantness that may be involved. Most dissatisfied customers don't express their dissatisfaction by complaining. Brand switching, patronage change, and purchase termination (often coupled with bad-mouthing the product or company) are much more customary expressions of dissatisfaction. This is particularly so in markets where competition is intense, many alternative suppliers are available, and where the products don't involve much emotional or financial commitment for the consumer.

Obviously, it is very difficult through complaint analysis to determine whether the opinions in the complaint are shared by a greater number of customers and whether they warrant management action in terms of altering or terminating a product, company policy, marketing program, advertising copy, etc. But they are early warning signals— quicker than marketing research and less costly than customer defection. Complaints hint at potential market problems; marketing research would be well advised to use complaints as a starting point in the search for causes and to correct mistakes.

The market's way of telling the firm about its failures is brutal and brief. Not only are complaints less costly to handle but they also give the seller a chance to recover. The seller may learn something as well. I remember a cosmetics company that received complaints about sticky sun block lotion. At the time, all such lotions were more or less sticky, so the risk of having customers go to competition was not great. But this was also an opportunity. The company managed to develop a product that was not sticky and captured 20 percent of the market in its first year. Another company had the opposite problem. Its products were not sticky enough. The company was a Royal Post Office in Europe and the product was a stamp. The problem was that the stamp didn't stick to the envelope. Management contacted the stamp producer who made it clear that if people just moistened the stamps properly, they would stick to any piece of paper. What to do? Management didn't take long to come to the conclusion that it would be more costly to try to educate its customers in stamp licking than to add more glue. The stamp producer was so instructed and the problem didn't occur again.

Since it is in the interest of the firm to have buyers complain rather than go elsewhere, it is important to make it easier for and, as a matter of fact, encourage dissatisfied customers to complain. Too many companies do the opposite—reducing complaint volume by making complaining costly, difficult, or unpleasant. One common approach for minimizing complaints is the automated customer service 1–800 number, where a computerized telephone system routes customers from one automatic menu to the next, making customers' attempt to talk to a person futile. With the possible exception for monopolies, this type of complaint handling only saves costs that are recorded. The unrecorded costs will be greater as dissatisfied customers leave for competition.

Our research has shown that if complaints are well managed, the complaining customer may become a loyal customer. In addition, we will learn about problems that need resolutions. So that other customers may be spared. Yet, our data also show that most companies treat complainers so poorly that there is an adverse impact on repeat business. Of all the industries included in the ACSI, only supermarkets seem to do a reasonably good job resolving customer complaints. Hospitals seem to be the worst offenders. Life insurance, airlines, and health insurance are not far behind. Strangely enough, household appliance makers, which do very well in terms of customer satisfaction, are only marginally better at handling complaints than cable TV companies (which are among the lowest-scoring businesses in customer satisfaction). Although no individual company stands out with respect to complaint management, luxury automobile nameplates dominate the list of top complaint management. Overall, six of the top ten complaint-handling companies are automobile manufacturers. The chart below shows how various industries do on complaint handling as measured by the ACSI (on a 0–100 scale, ranked from worst to best).

Table 6.1   National ACSI Complaint Handling by Industry

Industry	2002	2003	2004	2005	2006	5 Year AVG (0–100)
Hospitals	43	45	34	38	39	**40**
Life Insurance	48	44	51	47	34	**45**
E-Commerce: Auction	39	51	48	48	45	**46**
Airlines	50	51	44	46	46	**47**
Healthcare Insurance	51	44	50	48	51	**49**
Internet News & Information	60	51	45	33	56	**49**
Energy Utilities	54	52	53	51	51	**52**
Personal Computer	56	54	50	52	54	**53**
Personal Property Insurance	50	55	54	54	53	**53**
Fixed Line Telephone Service	53	57	54	52	55	**54**
E-Commerce: Brokerage	50	58	62	52	58	**56**
Express Delivery	64	51	58	53	58	**57**
E-Commerce: Retail	60	52	53	62	61	**58**

Continued

Table 6.1 Continued

Industry	2002	2003	2004	2005	2006	5 Year AVG (0–100)
Cable & Satellite Television	54	59	60	58	59	**58**
Hotel Industry	61	61	58	59	56	**59**
Household Appliances	60	61	60	60	55	**59**
Department and Discount Stores	55	59	59	62	62	**59**
Banks	61	61	61	57	59	**60**
Limited Service Restaurants	60	61	NM	58	62	**60**
Specialty Retail Stores	61	68	58	57	58	**60**
Newspaper Publishing Industry	68	62	68	59	56	**62**
Automobiles	65	63	62	64	63	**63**
Supermarkets	69	76	66	61	71	**68**

In quite a few service businesses we found that customers who canceled their service were roughly 50 percent more likely to have registered a complaint than customers who didn't cancel. Among customers with a problem, the process of resolving the problem is usually the dominant driver of satisfaction and loyalty. The biggest problems in complaint handling seem to be:

- Slow resolution of the problem;
- Partial resolution of the problem; and
- No follow-up to make sure the problem has been resolved.

For most companies, follow-up is haphazard at best. Either the proper systems are not in place or the volume of complaints is too high. Customers tend to be forgiving up to a point. For follow-up, most simply want to know that they're not forgotten. A simple procedure would be to provide a callback to any event not marked as resolved within one week of the customer complaint, and to make sure that procedure is known to the customer.

But beyond establishing clear protocols and internal alerts for following up with a customer, how to best balance a *quick* response with a *complete* response? Obviously, both would be best. But what if that's not possible? Figure 6.1 shows satisfaction scores by the length of time it took for the company to respond. Not surprisingly, those who received a response the same day are the most satisfied, while those who received a response three days later are less so. Faster is better. No surprise here. But if we look at customers who had their problem resolved successfully and compare them to those who did not, it is clear that substance trumps speed no matter what. Better to take time to resolve an issue than to get back quickly without a resolution.

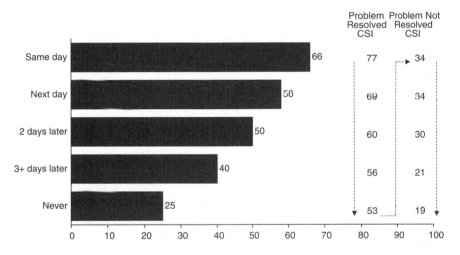

Figure 6.1   Customer Satisfaction and Response Time

Source: American Customer Satisfaction Index

In today's information age, failing to address a customer's complaint can have large repercussions. That's what the DoubleTree Club hotel discovered when a couple of web consultants from Seattle arrived well after midnight at a DoubleTree Club hotel in Houston, Texas. Both men had made guaranteed reservations in advance of their trip and secured rooms with major credit cards. Additionally, when making the reservations, they had informed the hotel that they would be arriving very late because of their travel schedule. One of them was a Gold VIP with Hilton Hotels (the parent company of DoubleTree), a regular and preferred customer, and so neither had a second thought about the availability of their rooms, regardless of the lateness of their arrival.

Much to their dismay, however, when they arrived at the front desk, they were informed that their rooms were no longer available and that the only empty rooms in the entire hotel were uninhabitable for one reason or another—broken plumbing or malfunctioning air conditioners. The night clerk seemed not terribly concerned. Although he appeared to recognize that their rooms had been incorrectly given to other guests, nothing was done to find alternate accommodations. This was the fault of the travelers themselves: "Most of our guests don't arrive at two o'clock in the morning." After debating the interpretation of the word "guaranteed" with the clerk, the two saw little change in attitude—there was nothing to apologize for, according to the night clerk. The two men eventually found rooms at a discount hotel several miles away.

This story is not exceptional, and doesn't deserve much discussion except for one thing. Since I don't know the two travelers, how did I learn about their experience? And why bother writing about it? Bad customer service is commonplace. But unlike most tales of this kind, this story did become quite well-known. After all, we are talking about web consultants here. They can be dangerous customers if ticked off. And, in this case, they did not take their mistreatment lightly. Instead, what happened made it into their laptops and created a scathing PowerPoint presentation, "Yours is a Very Bad Hotel," detailing the experiences of Tom and Shane. One of the men e-mailed the presentation to his mother and a few others, and from there, it spread like wild fire. Linked, copied, and plastered all over the Internet, Tom and Shane's story of poor customer service became notorious . In an age of consumer generated media, the story became "viral," spreading across the web and getting a huge audience. A decade or so ago, Tom and Shane's adventure would have moved a very limited distance, if at all, and dissipated quickly. Today, a bad customer service incident can become an international phenomenon. Many news stories were written about Tom and Shane's experiences and their approach for seeking redress. In fact, "Yours is a Very Bad Hotel" became so well-known that the two web consultants were overwhelmed by the publicity and media inquiries, hired a PR firm, held a "Netcast" to discuss their experiences, and, consequently, received copious public apologies from DoubleTree and its parent company, Hilton. The DoubleTree hotel was swamped with bad press and apparently used this case as a starting point for hotel service improvements.

There is a standard practice in business that the validity of a complaint should be ascertained before any compensation is provided to the complainant. This practice is often counterproductive. Let's do the math: Suppose that a company has received 30,000 complaints and that it costs $25 on average to investigate whether a complaint is valid or not. On the other hand, compensating each complaining customer, without any investigation whatsoever, would cost $50 per customer, on the average. If all complaints are investigated, the cost would be $750,000. The total compensation, without investigation, would be $1.5 million. But suppose that 60 percent of complaints turn out to be valid, reflecting deficiencies in a product or service requiring redress. For 40 percent of our complaining customers, we have expended $300,000 to investigate. We found no cause for compensation. For 60 percent of our customers, we have expended $450,000 to investigate. We determined these complaints to be valid. The compensation cost for these customers amounts to $900,000. Now, we have $300,000 + $450,000 + $900,000 = $1.65 million. This is more than the $1.5 million we could have spent by compensating customers if we did not investigate. Coupled with the fact that we would have responded faster, gained customer's goodwill and loyalty, the investigation approach seems very unattractive.

What about cheating, one might object. If one has a lot of dishonest customers, perhaps it wouldn't be optimal to pay complainant compensation without looking into the legitimacy of the matter. But even here, it doesn't matter much who's right and who's wrong. The economics of complaint management is concerned with one thing: What's the economic value of the complaining customer? It is that value, and the extent to which it can be affected by complaint management, that determines the break-even point for compensation.

DON'T EXCEED CUSTOMER EXPECTATIONS

One of the most common excuses for waning satisfaction is the myth of rising expectations. The logic goes something like this: Product quality always improves. Customers have come to expect more and more from their suppliers and expectations rise much faster than quality.

But ACSI data suggest that customer expectations are essentially rational and adaptive in the face of changing market conditions. The implication is that aggregate expectations are reasonably well synchronized with the quality that products and services actually deliver. In the case of repeat purchasing, the consumer relies on his/her previous consumption experiences. Unless there is a great variation in quality over time, these expectations should not be far off the mark. If satisfaction is high, expectations are likely to be high as well; likewise, if satisfaction is low, expectations tend to adjust downward. I am a frequent flyer—my work takes me around the world on a regular basis. Satisfaction with airlines is near the bottom, but passenger expectations are not high either. I expect long waits, crowded planes, less than excellent food, and you know what? Most airlines meet my expectations—sometime they exceed them (not by much, but things are sometimes better). But that doesn't mean that I'm a satisfied passenger: Even though most airlines meet my expectations, my *standards* for being a satisfied passenger are not the same as my *expectations*. The latter are predictions about the level of service that I am about to experience.

Things are different for first-time purchases. By definition, the first time we buy a particular product, we have no prior experience with that product. Other sources of information, advertising, and promotion play a larger role. Yet here, too, there are forces balancing expectations. If sellers exaggerate product claims, a one-time purchase may be gained but only at the expense of a long-term customer. If, on the other hand, the seller downplays the excellence of its product in order to create low expectations, chances are that there won't be a purchase in the first place. Thus, there is a system of "checks and balances" that constrains a seller's incentive to either exaggerate claims or deflate expectations.

This doesn't mean, however, that we should seek to exceed our customers' expectations. Although the idea of exceeding expectations may sound good as a business slogan, it's not good business. It's no more realistic than it is for firms to continually exceed financial expectations. Since customer expectations are largely rational and buyers rapidly learn (and remember) what to expect, we would create even higher expectations for the next purchase. This is especially risky in services where satisfaction is highly dependent on personalized service. Companies that have excellent service staff and high levels of customer satisfaction will find that more efforts directed at exceeding expectations often come close to the point of diminishing returns, just as in the case of maximizing satisfaction. Customer expectations should be met, but generally not exceeded.

For instance, a large retail department store learned that checkout wait times had a substantial impact on customer satisfaction. If customers had to wait more than 60 seconds at the register (and it didn't matter if it was 65 or 90 seconds), they would become upset and dissatisfied. Conversely, wait times of 30 to 60 seconds were acceptable, though 30 was clearly more acceptable than 60. It was thought that if customers were happy with a 30-second wait, they would be thrilled with a 20-second wait. But customers were perfectly willing to wait for 30 seconds and even somewhat longer, and attending to them more quickly was of no consequence whatsoever. Yet the company wasted time and money on extra cashiers to exceed expectations and reduce average wait times to 20 seconds. Customers simply weren't any more satisfied and thus didn't buy more or became more loyal customers. The retailer exceeded expectations, but at a loss of profit.

MERGERS AND ACQUISITIONS: WHAT HAPPENS TO THE CUSTOMER ASSET?

Mergers and acquisitions can be an instant shot in the arm to pump up the kind of immediate growth that gets Wall Street excited. Having trouble growing your firm? Looking for cost efficiencies to be found in economies of scale? Are customers defecting to competition and earnings beginning to suffer? Not to worry, just buy those customers back by acquiring the competition. There's just one problem: 70 percent to 80 percent of all acquisitions fail, and, as a result, firms end up losing the very shareholders they seek to please, destroying wealth in the process. A few years ago Larry Selden and Geoffrey Colvin studied $12 trillion worth in M&A and concluded that at least $1 trillion in shareholder value was destroyed.[4]

One reason most acquisitions fail to generate shareholder wealth is that they often leave customers worse off. Our data show that customer satisfaction and shareholder value generally go together. Satisfied customers tend to provide more repeat business and generate a stable income stream. In terms of both revenue and profit, most of this stream comes from repeat business and repeat business is highly dependent on having satisfied customers. Why does the customer relationship suffer in the wake of many mergers and acquisitions? There are several reasons:

- Cost-cutting and streamlining leading to fewer alternatives, whether brands or retail outlets;
- Cost efficiencies that reduce customer service;

- Difficulties in coordinating and working together; and
- Not understanding the customers of the acquired company.

Most of these problems affected customers of CompuServe when it was acquired by America Online (AOL) in 1998. Today, a decade later, problems still remain. Consider what happened to Marilyn McDuff of Santa Rosita, California. She mailed in a check for her dial-up Internet access through CompuServe as she had done every month for the past two years. The difference this time was that it was to be the last payment, as Marilyn had arranged to cancel her service. CompuServe had been bought by AOL to add to its own subscription based dial-up service. That's when the trouble began. AOL integrated the two companies' billing processes into a new automated system designed to handle both sets of customers. What Marilyn didn't expect was that this new system would lose her check. She had mailed it to the CompuServe billing address, but apparently the check did not get to where it needed to go. Fast forward several months. No past due notices had come in the mail to alert Marilyn that something might be amiss when a phone call came from a debt collector. As part of the integration process with AOL, delinquent accounts were flagged and this one showed up as past due. Still, Marilyn didn't panic, thinking a quick phone call and the matter would be cleared up. But it wasn't. She called AOL only to find out that since she had been a CompuServe customer she needed to contact CompuServe. But CompuServe couldn't track the history since the account had been merged into AOL's billing system, so back Marilyn was sent to AOL. And this went on for over a year with phone calls to AOL and CompuServe, and letters back and forth between the two organizations. Not only had the check been lost, but the account itself could not be found either. The matter remained unresolved for almost ten years (although officially the debt was written off). Not coincidentally perhaps, AOL received the lowest satisfaction score of any company recorded by the ACSI.

Layoffs and closed-out franchise locations may be profitable short-term consequences of M&A, but they tend to have adverse long-term consequences. They often damage customer relationships in a number of ways—ranging from simple confusion over which firm is the customer's provider to turnover in front-line personnel and in management. Many industries were heavily involved in the merger wave of the mid to late 1990s. Two worth noting are commercial banks and fixed-line telecommunications firms. The former has seen merger activity slack considerably after 2000, the latter never really stopped. Major national banks spent the last half of the 1990s gobbling up large and small competitors alike, reducing competition, opening up new markets and increasing total assets all at the same time. But customer relationships deteriorated. Customer satisfaction with banks took a steep dive in the midst of the merger activity.

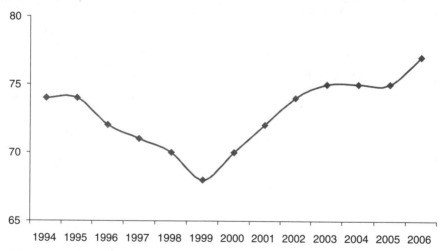

Figure 6.2 ACSI Commercial Banks 1994 to 2006

Branches changed names overnight and others closed entirely. ATM locations, where many Americans do all of their banking, vanished or changed owners, and mix-ups with various automated systems related to customer accounts were frequent. Just as the rash of mergers had caused satisfaction to plummet through 2000, slowing of M&A activity coincided with an equally strong upswing in satisfaction with banks. And the more recent acquisitions of Fleet Boston Financial Corporation by Bank of America and Bank One by J. P. Morgan Chase didn't have the usual adverse effects. While it is probably too early to speculate on this, it seems that banks may have learned a lesson and now handle their mergers with more attention to the customer asset.

A quarter century after AT&T was forced to break up its local telephone systems into seven Baby Bells, it now looks like the number of competitors has shrunk to the point where we are back to the era before de-regulation with many fewer providers.

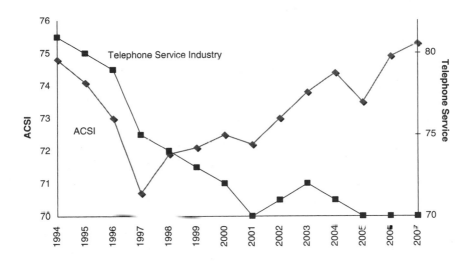

Figure 6.3 Telephone Service Merger and Declining Satisfaction

Source: American Customer Satisfaction Index

The story of how seven Baby Bells became three is a long and complicated one. It started in 1997 when one of the "babies," Bell Atlantic, acquired its regional neighbor, sibling NYNEX. Then Southwestern Bell

Communications (SBC) acquired Pacific Telesis in 1998 and added another sibling, Ameritech, in 1999. In 2000, U.S. West was bought by newcomer Qwest Communications, while, at the same time, Bell Atlantic and GTE, the largest of the independent telephone companies during the Baby Bell era, merged to form Verizon. At this point customer satisfaction reached a record low. What's kept it low is that the merger saga didn't come to an end. Satisfaction improved slightly for a couple of years after the first spate of mergers ended, but more mergers and a drop in satisfaction soon followed. SBC returned to roots in 2005, when it bought its own parent AT&T and took its name. The new AT&T then purchased Bell South in 2006, with Cingular Wireless as part of the deal, also to be renamed AT&T. And just for good measure, Verizon, the former Bell Atlantic that had acquired NYNEX, acquired the long-distance carrier MCI.

All this is not to suggest that mergers are always bad for shareholders because of deteriorating customer relationships and lower customer asset values. Sometimes they work. Banks seem to have figured out how. It's not all that difficult, at least not in principle. First, be realistic. How will the balance sheet look in terms of return on invested capital? Capital invested goes up, often dramatically, so even if profit follows, it may be an expensive proposition in terms of return on capital. Second, look beyond the balance sheet and consider the implications for the value of the customer relationships. Very little effort appears to have been made in this regard. Millions of dollars are spent to determine the value of target companies. I have yet to see any comprehensive analysis about the value of customer assets or the impact of this value after the acquisition. Curiously enough, mergers often take place between firms that don't have very high customer satisfaction, or when the target company has weak customer relationships. In both situations, the value of the combined customer asset will suffer, sometimes for years after the deal. We've already seen how Sprint's acquisition of Nextel diminished the customer asset and adversely affected the newly formed company's financials. Daimler's acquisition of Chrysler is another example. Daimler purchased Chrysler in 1998 for $36 billion and sold it in 2007 for $7.4 billion.

WHAT'S PRICE GOT TO DO
WITH IT? VERY LITTLE!

Kmart Corporation was facing a bleak future heading into the final quarter of 2001. The number three discount retailer in the United States behind Wal-Mart and Target, Kmart had been consistently below average in customer satisfaction. With earnings falling throughout the 1990s, Kmart began shedding operations, selling or spinning off most of its retail assets, including the Borders bookstore chain and office supply retailer OfficeMax, and closing more than 200 of its Kmart stores. Still, it wasn't enough to stop the financial bleeding—the retailer's problems were rooted in a history of poor quality merchandise and inferior service.

Heading into the fourth quarter of 2001, the most important time period in retailing with the huge holiday shopping season looming, the situation for Kmart had become dire. Watching sales plunge and seeing its customers defect in large numbers in favor of Target and Wal-Mart, Kmart slashed prices across the board in an effort to rejuvenate sales and stave off bankruptcy. The prices struck some customers as almost too good to be true—a kid's bike for five dollars! As management had forecasted, customer satisfaction improved quickly and dramatically, as did customers' perceptions of value, and Kmart enjoyed a temporary bump-up in sales. But the improvement was short-lived. When prices returned to normal levels after the holiday shopping season, satisfaction fell, most new customers returned to their preferred shopping places, and Kmart was in an even worse position than before. The price discounting was so deep that margins were sometimes negative and the super low prices didn't help the company overcome the negative perceptions of Kmart quality. In January 2002, many key suppliers suspended shipments Kmart could no longer pay. Faced with the prospect of dwindling inventory, Kmart's fate was sealed. The company filed Chapter 11 bankruptcy protection. Price is almost always a double-edged sword.

What happened to Kmart is typical for a company that competes on price but doesn't have the resources to keep it low enough. As a result, it resorts to temporary price promotions. Both quality and price are important determinants of customer satisfaction, but quality has much more leverage. There is not much to be gained in satisfaction or repeat business from a buyer who purchases at a price discount. As is typical of similar situations, the temporary price reductions used by Kmart had detrimental effects. Because they were temporary, the customers were temporary too. If price discounting causes a buyer to switch from a favorite supplier to a discounted product, that buyer is more likely to return to the preferred supplier unless offered more (and steeper) future discounts. Market share captured by lowering price doesn't always translate into higher customer satisfaction, and unless the seller is capable of sustained discounting, such share gains are difficult to protect.

Wal-Mart is different. It is so large that it has a great deal of power over suppliers. Any supplier would hesitate to give up distribution of its merchandise through the largest retailer in the world. With enough volume, they may still make money. With the ability to dictate lower wholesale costs from suppliers, Wal-Mart can undercut competition on its retail pricing and still maintain profit margins. But Wal-Mart is an exception. Only companies that have strong cost advantages can successfully compete on price to the extent Wal-Mart can. Companies at a competitive cost disadvantage—like the U.S. auto makers—cannot play this game. They tried and paid a big price: Market share has been eroding steadily.

In 1970, the Big Three U.S. car manufacturers had 87 percent of the U.S. auto market. By 2005, that share had fallen to 57 percent and it is anticipated that by 2008, foreign automobiles will make up slightly more than half of all sales in the United States. There are only two ways in which cost disadvantages can be overcome. Either productivity has to be increased or customer satisfaction needs to be improved. Otherwise, it will be very difficult to be competitive. But for

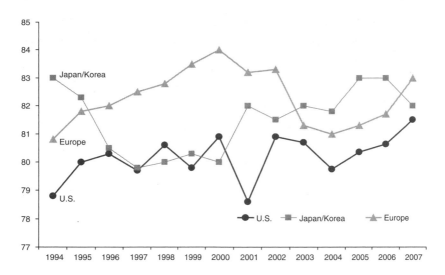

Figure 6.4 ACSI of Domestic and International Nameplates, 1994 to 2007*

* Mercedes-Benz is treated as European.
Source: American Customer Satisfaction Index

the past seven years, customer satisfaction with U.S. car makers remains behind competition even though it has improved since 2004.

The problem is that much of the increased satisfaction has been achieved through buyer price incentives. Rebates, low cost, zero-percent financing, and employee discounts to the public have halted sales erosion and helped customer satisfaction for U.S. automakers, but they have also taken a toll on profits. In contrast, the rising satisfaction with non-U.S. cars is due to improvements in quality and customization. Price promotions usually, but not always, have a positive effect on customer satisfaction, but it is generally not large or sustainable.

It is still unclear if Detroit is taking customer satisfaction, or the lack thereof, seriously enough. Measurement procedures are primitive, problems are not well identified, and across-the-board price-cutting to reduce inventory has become standard. In contrast, industry leader Toyota has been raising prices. Rising customer satisfaction shifts the demand curve upward, making room for price increases.

Falling customer satisfaction, or satisfaction caused by price reductions, has the opposite effect. But perhaps there is hope. At the January 2006 Detroit Auto Show, then Ford CEO Bill Ford announced that "from now on, our products will be designed and built to satisfy the customer, not just to fill a factory." The question is, what took them so long? Perhaps it's too little, too late, but there are some encouraging signs for Detroit: Since 2006, customer satisfaction is generally up and the improvements are not due to price discounts, but better product quality.

CUSTOMER LOYALTY CAN BE BOUGHT— SATISFACTION MUST BE EARNED

Long-term customer relationships are characterized by efficiency, low risk, and predictable revenue. The general theory for creating such relationships in a market economy is clear enough. Sellers compete for buyers' preference and satisfaction. Winners are rewarded by lower cost and lower risk, by returning customers, and by a favorable treatment from equity markets. These are the basic rule of a free market system. In an increasingly time-pressured environment, where managers are responsible for innumerable processes, people, and objectives, the rules of the game are occasionally forgotten. For example, it is sometimes said that customer satisfaction is "worthless" but loyalty is "priceless" or that trying to satisfy the customer can be a "trap" for business. The reasoning is that customer satisfaction doesn't always lead to repeat business. This is true, but misses the point. Customer loyalty *without* satisfaction not only confuses means with ends, but also contradicts how free markets operate. Take Cuba or North Korea, for example. They don't have free markets, but they do have a great deal of customer loyalty without much customer satisfaction.

Obviously, not all satisfied customers will buy again, but that's not a reason for abandoning efforts on customer satisfaction in favor of loyalty. Loyalty is an objective of the seller—buyers are not particularly interested in it. Customer-centered organizations accomplish their objectives by understanding what buyers want. Take H&R Block, for example. Even though the firm has not done well for its shareholders during the last five years, its ten-year performance has been spectacular. Once it has a new customer, managers know that the next three years are critical. Not that H&R Block has the luxury of three years to prove what it can do, but this is the period during which customer trust is either developed or it doesn't materialize. If customers are satisfied with the services after about three years, the relationship tends to become stable and mature. The economics that follow are substantial, for seller as well as for buyer. Even in the case of a service failure, the customer who has a long history with H&R Block is more apt to dismiss it as a mishap. This is true for most firms under most circumstances.

There are other ways to generate customer loyalty, but they are more expensive. Loyalty can always be bought via price and price discounts. In the short term, it is not always easy to avoid this strategy, as witnessed by the U.S. automobile industry. Until recently, H&R Block has managed, by and large, to avoid it. Instead, it attempts to earn client loyalty by putting client satisfaction at a premium. Tax preparers strive to be proactive in offering information to their clients about the process, timing, status, and ways to get information. They call clients after the filing to let them know the status of the tax return. For H&R Block, one of the strongest drivers of customer satisfaction, and subsequent loyalty, is similitude of tax preparer. It is essential that the customer gets the same tax preparer from year to year. Thus in the case of H&R Block, the value of the customer relationships hinges to a great extent on another intangible asset: the employees. In order to insure that the tax filer gets the same preparer, H&R Block puts a great deal of effort into personnel retention. Turnover is about 20 percent, which is lower than the national average for American companies but still quite costly for a firm like H&R Block.

Loyalty obviously has a strong correlation with revenue (it is almost the same thing), but revenue is not always a good business objective. As many of the airlines, car makers, computer, and telecommunication firms have found out, customer loyalty can come at a high cost, especially if not coupled with high customer satisfaction. The only way to keep a customer who is not particularly satisfied and has a choice is to offer a price deal. Hence, only deal-prone customers are retained (only to be lost to anybody that offers a better deal the next time), and profit margins evaporate. The result is a periodic trading of non-profitable customers among competitors. In fact, all our empirical research findings show that customer satisfaction has a stronger effect on financial performance than does loyalty. The reason is that the increased revenue generated by improved loyalty is not offset by the higher cost unless that loyalty is generated by growing customer satisfaction.

I have heard several management consulting companies pronounce that customer loyalty is more important than customer satisfaction. That's dangerous advice. In a competitive marketplace, especially one in which the customer is becoming more empowered, failing to satisfy one's customers is a precursor to being kicked out of business. Although a satisfied customer may or may not come back for more, the probability of repeat business is much higher for a satisfied customer than it is for a customer who is dissatisfied. Customer loyalty is different. It is a behavior. As such, it is a consequence of something. It is very difficult to manage consequences. Good management is about affecting the causes of consequences, not the consequence themselves.

So what is loyalty a consequence of? Three things: the satisfaction of the customer, the barriers to switching from one supplier to another, and price. These things can be managed.

CHAPTER 7

Customer Asset Management: Offense Versus Defense

CFI started as a way for me to organize my time and be able to better respond to requests from businesses about how to best measure customer satisfaction and predict its financial consequences. Between research and teaching MBAs, it was difficult to find time. Today, CFI has offices on several continents and its sister company, Foresee Results, is growing rapidly. It's a far cry from the days when I would staple presentations myself. But even today, we don't do a great deal of marketing. But we get even more calls from organizations in both the private and public sector. A few years ago, the CEO of a very successful online firm contacted us because his firm's customers were defecting at an alarming rate. For every customer won, the company was losing an average of 1.3 customers. This was new and it was scary—anybody could do the math and see where the company was heading. For that, they didn't need our expertise.

This company had grown very fast and now has a customer base in the millions. The business itself was a fairly ubiquitous rental service. But its appeal was an online service delivery that was quick, inexpensive, and much more efficient than what other companies had been able to provide. Revenues had doubled nearly every year and the company won high praise from Wall Street; it weathered the dot-com bubble burst, and looked to most observers destined for long-term success. But what was happening now was right out of the text book. Business pioneering and early advantage only last so long. It took the more established companies some time to awaken, but when they did it was like a bear in spring: They were lean, mean, and hungry, with a good deal of strength left. The established brick-and-mortar retailers whose business the upstart had invaded and ravaged for several years now had caught on and were fighting back. Not only had they learned to do a better job protecting their customers from competitive inroads, but they were also having much more success in taking away business from the pure e-tailers. And things were moving fast.

But there was nothing particularly creative or novel about what was going on. Prediction is not difficult if you have a bit of history and theory as a guide. Sure, you might still be wrong, but chances are that the systematic part of history will repeat itself. All you have to figure out is what's systematic and what's random. The "old" competition adapted gradually by copying the online business model and simply adding direct-to-consumer rental options. The customers didn't need to go to a physical location. More effort was also directed at operations of the core business by better measuring customer satisfaction, identifying old-standing customer irritants and removing them, working to better match the needs of different segments in service offerings, and—what caused much damage to the less well-financed upstarts—price cutting. The CEO who contacted us realized that he was getting a taste of his own medicine. To make matters worse, his company was also being squeezed from the other side, with new business imitators popping-up, beginning to take a share of market as well. The question was: What to do in order to stop the bleeding?

Through our discussions, the nature of the company's primary objectives became clearer. Here was a company that had always been on the offensive. Now it needed a good defense. The offense is about getting new customers. Offensive strategies seek to take market share from competition, encourage brand switching and increase purchase frequency. Defensive strategy is about reducing customer defection and brand switching. Its objective is to minimize customer turnover by protecting customers from competitors' attempts to lure them away.

But it is not easy to switch from offense to defense. It requires a different mindset, different management principles, different marketing, and a different way of doing sales. There was no mystery about what was wrong with our e-tailer and what needed to be done to turn things around. Above all, the company needed to reduce customer churn. Customer acquisition was costly and it didn't seem to be getting less expensive over time. It called for large price incentives and big advertising budgets. Under such conditions, the guiding principle must be to prevent competitors from taking away business.

To be sure, this story is far from unique. The globalization of consumer markets and the Internet itself has led to many opportunities, but most of them also come with challenges in the form of new sources of competition. The proliferation of new communications technologies has brought consumers many more choices. *Time Magazine*'s 2006 person of the year was "everyone," the logic being that the average person in the Information Age is much more empowered today than was the case a few years ago.

How do you successfully compete in a hyper-competitive and constantly evolving environment? How could this e-commerce firm avoid being more than a short-term novelty and convert early success into sustainable business? Where can a company find solutions to these challenges? How do we identify the customers we are likely to keep, those we are at risk of losing, and those almost certain to defect? How can we determine which customers are too expensive to keep? What is a customer worth, anyway? And how can we most efficiently market to new customers, discovering those customers we have a better shot at winning, and especially those customers who are more likely to remain loyal—and be more profitable—over time? The answers to these questions lie in Customer Asset Management (CAM).

The idea behind CAM is that we manage the company as a portfolio of customers. Customer satisfaction is managed such that its positive effects (repeat business, high reservation prices, cross selling, etc.) are captured, and the harmful effects of a discontented buyer are minimized. CAM is about measuring, developing, and nurturing customer relationships. Of course, it's the relationships—the bond, glue, tie, or whatever we may want to call them—that are economic assets, not the customers themselves. And it is the sum of the value of these assets that comprise the value of the firm. Accordingly, the principles behind CAM are:

- satisfied customers are an economic asset that yields future cash flows;
- this cash flow can be expressed as net present value;
- costs incurred to build the customer asset base are investments—not expenses; and
- good management of customer assets is critical for long-term profitability.

This means that through CAM we get:

- a monetary estimate of the value of the customer asset;
- a diagnosis of what to do to increase its value;
- a linkage back to operations, processes, and personnel; and
- a linkage forward to future cash flows and asset appreciation.

In other words, Customer Asset Management should inform us where we are, where we should go, how to get there, and what happens when we do get there.

The question of where we are may seem straightforward. But in many cases, it isn't. There are businesses where management doesn't know who its customers are. Take the household appliance industry, for example. Swedish company AB Electrolux is the world's largest producer of household appliances, selling washing machines, stoves, refrigerators, and freezers under a variety of brand names. The company has been quite savvy about acquiring well-placed competitors, and has expanded aggressively into new markets over the past decade. But in the mid-1990s, the situation for Electrolux was different. The company was not performing to expectations, and as part of its restructuring plan, which included closing about two dozen plants and eliminating more than 10,000 jobs, we worked with its management to improve customer satisfaction.

Electrolux knew very, very little about its own customers. How could a large, very successful consumer goods manufacturer not know its customers well? For a company like Electrolux, the answer is simple. Electrolux, much like many durable goods manufacturers, relies mostly on third-party retail outlets to sell its products. Since there was no effective way to reach Electrolux customers, we did the next best thing: We measured the satisfaction of the retailers who sold Electrolux appliances. In many ways, distributors and retailers can be looked upon as proxies for the end user. In this case, it worked out very well because the retailers knew a great deal that Electrolux didn't about its customers. Knowing the sources of revenue and profits is the hallmark of customer orientation. But Electrolux is not alone in having difficulty tracking it.

In principle, there are only two ways in which we can keep customers: by providing strong customer satisfaction or by creating switching barriers. It is helpful to have a bit of both. A switching barrier is anything that would make it difficult, costly, cumbersome, or illegal for a customer to switch from one supplier to another. Is it costly to switch from a PC to a Mac? From Verizon to Sprint? From Club Med to Sandals?

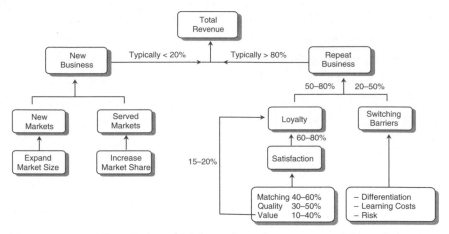

Figure 7.1 The Role of Value, Satisfaction, and Loyalty

Source: American Customer Satisfaction Index

For airlines, frequent flyer programs are a switching barrier—an economic incentive with the purpose of discouraging passenger switching. Most successful companies have switching barriers to some extent. However, the switching barrier, while it may be good defensively, it is not so good for the offense. If the buyer is aware of the switching barriers before the purchase is made, the offense becomes more difficult.

Surprisingly few companies keep track of customers lost, gained, and retained. But it's critical to do so. Customer retention can be measured in several ways, but all relate in one way or another to the proportion of customers (or accounts) retained per time period (a year, quarter, etc.). For many companies, 70 to 80 percent of the total revenue represents the proportion from repeat business. Suppose Volvo cars have 70 percent customer retention. That is, 70 percent of the current Volvo owners will buy a Volvo next time. What happens if we could increase that number by two—for a customer retention rate of 72 percent instead of 70 percent? In other words, if Volvo invested in customer satisfaction and, because of the increasing satisfaction, customer retention moved up to 72 percent, what's the return on that investment? Let's begin in the simplest manner possible, without considering present value analysis, profit margins, time horizons, or retention probability distributions. If 70 percent of my customers return, how many purchases would they give me? Since I am losing 30 percent of my customers each purchase cycle, the average customer would be worth 70/30 = 2.3 purchases. At 72 percent customer retention, the average customer would be worth 72/28 = 2.7 purchases. That is, 0.4 more purchases. That's a gain of 17 percent. So an improvement by 2 percentage points in customer retention produces a 17 percent increase in the value of the customer asset, measured as volume of purchases over time. Unless it's going to cost me a great deal to accomplish this, it seems like a pretty nice return.

Now, let's look at banks. Some have a 90 percent retention rate per year. Consequently, they lose 10 percent of their customers per year. Suppose now that a typical bank also succeeded in holding onto an additional 2 percent of its current customers, bringing the customer retention rate to 92 percent. That's an increase in the value of the customer asset by 28 percent. Note that the value of 90 percent retention is an average of nine years in terms of customer lifetime value to the company. But a small increase of 2 percentage points to 92 percent (92/8 = 11.5) gives us 11.5 years. Thus, we have a 28 percent gain. Now that's a formidable increase. It is also easy to understand. Customer retention is one of those curves that have increasing returns. It's not quite as simple as my examples here but it's not that much more complicated either. The higher the customer retention rate, the higher the return from a further increase. But, rising cost will temper this a bit. It might be very difficult to keep a higher and higher proportion of customers. At some point, it will probably cost us more than it is worth.

But there are exceptions to every rule. Foresee Results, which measures customer satisfaction for websites and provides diagnostics for how to best improve these sites, has a customer retention rate of 129 percent. "How can you keep more than 100 percent of your customers?" I asked Larry Freed, the CEO of Foresee. "Sounds like a mathematical impossibility to me." "It depends on what you count,"

Larry explained. "We're counting dollars per account, not accounts per se." Not only does Foresee have a high customer retention rate, its customers also keep buying more services. This is the ultimate in customer retention economics.

To get a more precise estimate of the value of customer assets, one needs to take profit margins, the time horizon, and the cost of money into account. Sunil Gupta and Don Lehmann discuss this in some detail, but they nevertheless conclude that customer retention is the key factor.[1] It has a much greater effect than the discount rate and the time horizon. There are many models for estimating the customer lifetime value in the technical literature.[2] Obviously, profit margins can have a great effect, but they may vary over the time horizon. In fact, profit margins may go up if highly satisfied customers are less costly to serve, less sensitive to price increases, and don't need as much reselling. But profit margins may go down if customers exercise more power and competition gets tougher.

The returns on customer retention explain why it is that firms with satisfied customers do much better financially than others. They also explain why it pays off to invest in such firms. Not only is the return greater, but the risk is smaller due to the stability of cash flows for loyal customers. Now then, how do we manage to increase customer retention, without attempting to monopolize, which is not only difficult but may have risky long-term consequences, and to refrain from lowering prices? Price can be used to gain more repeat business, but it's costly. It has a direct effect on profit margins: it often conditions the buyer to postpone and wait until there's a price deal. Price is often the weapon of last resort or a short term fix (that can be very expensive in the long run.) Sustainable price reductions are different, but can only be pulled off by companies with superior cost structures.

From all the data I have seen on the matter, the best way to reap the benefits of steady high levels of cash flow from repeat business would be to make sure that customer satisfaction is high and continually improved upon. What then determines customer satisfaction? That brings us to quality. Quality of service and quality of product. But quality means different things to different people. Unless quality improvements are reflected in better customer satisfaction, the return on the quality investment will be totally cost dependent. If the higher quality isn't associated with lower cost, it would be a losing proposition.

But what is the relationship between changes in quality, customer satisfaction, retention, and profitability? Often not what you may think. I was working on a project for one of the Big Three car companies in Detroit. The question was: What parts and functions of the car were causing customer discontent and subsequent customer defection? One way of getting answers to this question was asking customers to tell us what they didn't like. But such an approach doesn't yield much useful information. We could try to correlate how customers rate various aspects of quality to their overall satisfaction. That would not give us much useful information either. But, that's what most companies do—ask customers directly or correlating responses. So let me explain what's wrong with approaches like these.

For a particular nameplate and a certain car model, we identified the key driver of dissatisfaction to be the location of the air conditioner controls. Not the looks of the car, the engine, the ride, safety, reliability, or comfort. Had we asked customers directly, we would never have come up with this one. The same would be true for correlation analysis. I remember giving the presentation of our findings to a group of senior engineers. They were skeptical, to say the least. Most of them didn't believe me. How could it be that the location of air conditioner controls was more important than major issues such as comfort and reliability? The consensus among the engineers was that the findings couldn't possibly be right. Well, they were right but the engineers were also right. They were right about the fact that what we had identified was not the most important thing in a car. Far from it. Air conditioner controls are not even close in importance compared with many other things in a car. If asked, any customer would tell you that.

But, the engineers were wrong about something else. This is not a question about what's important. For airlines, the most important aspect to passengers is that the plane doesn't hit the ground too fast at some location other than the intended one. But that doesn't necessarily mean that airline safety is a priority for improving passenger satisfaction. Clearly, location of air conditioner controls will never be the most important thing in a car. But what we want to do is to pinpoint that which needs to be fixed in order to reduce dissatisfaction and increase satisfaction. I am talking about marginal effects and analysis here: How will y change if we change x? That is what's relevant. The reason that engine, comfort, and reliability did not emerge as "important" was that they were deemed fine by the customers and needed no improvement. No effort to improve in those areas would cause a significant change in terms of customer satisfaction.

In addition, one should make a distinction between first purchase and repeat purchase—the factors that make somebody buy the car the first time were of less relevance here. In a first purchase, most of us probably don't even think about where the air conditioner controls are. It's of no importance. But once we have used the car for some time, this particular feature may well take on some importance. If it is difficult to reach or inconvenient, it may well turn into an irritant that, combined with other factors, would reduce customer retention.

Let me give another example. Detroit, which is a city close to where I live, may not be the nicest city in the world, but it is not terribly bad either. Like other cities, it is important for Detroit to attract conventions because they bring in money. Not too long ago, Detroit hosted a large medical convention. Everything went smoothly and things were seemingly fine. But after the conference, the executive responsible for convention site selection announced that they would never again come back to Detroit. What went wrong? Had conventioners been mugged in the streets? Was it dangerous to go outside?

It was none of these things. It turned out that for the big luncheon, plastic tableware was used instead of the promised silver. That did it.

Small things can make a big difference. Big things make a difference, too. But it depends on whether we are playing defense or offense. Shifting from offense to defense usually brings at least some low-hanging fruit for easy picking. But in mature industries, all the low-hanging fruit has been picked. For the Haier Group in China, the multi-billion dollar home appliance manufacturer, there is no more low-hanging fruit. But it wasn't always so. I was visiting the beautiful coastal city of Qingdao, where the Haier Group headquarters are located, having dinner with Kesong Wu, the vice chairman. Haier is the world's fourth-largest home appliance maker, selling to more than 160 countries. It has 60,000 sales agents worldwide. It is also a highly sophisticated company and a world leader in integrated networked appliances and in digitalization with large integrated circuits.

Things were very different a little more than a decade earlier. In there 1980s, the Qingdao General Refrigerator Factory produced only a single model. Suffering from poor management and low productivity—there were times that production rarely surpassed 80 units in a month—the factory was deep in debt and was close to bankrupt. Mr. Wu told me that the first order of business was to change employee behavior. Employees obviously have something to do with customer satisfaction. Three new objectives were established. First, the employees had to show up on time. Second, they had to stop urinating on the floor. Third, they could not leave until the work day had ended. It would be difficult to find more low-hanging fruit than this. No need for measurement or for systems to figure out marginal returns.

The next day, I had a long discussion with Mianmian Yang. She too joined the Qingdao Refrigerator Factory before it became Haier, and later became its president and chairperson. She explained that Haier's success was due to the view of customers as the ultimate source of growth, no matter where these customers were—as long as Haier could execute what she called "one low and three high." The "one low" would be cost and the "three highs" would be value, quality, and growth. And the key to it all was customer satisfaction. The low-hanging fruit consisting of an uneducated and undisciplined work force was long gone. The question was now how to pick high-hanging fruit. Which ones should be picked first? This is a difficult challenge for any company. Intuitively, albeit often reluctantly, cheered on by consultants, many companies seem to embrace the idea of staying close to the customer. That's probably a good idea, but it's not good to get too close.

DON'T GET TOO CLOSE TO
THE CUSTOMER

We have worked with a large shipping company for many years where management considers customer satisfaction vital for long-term financial health but does not expect customers to "run" its business. The company's customer experience with delivery services, package handling, billing, claims handling, shipping services, and a host of other factors are monitored quarterly and translated into business practice. That doesn't mean that the company acts on what customers view as important. Many aspects of the business are important to customers, but only a few are important in a marginal sense. The question is: How can we best improve aspects of our service and get the greatest effect on customer satisfaction improvement? In fact, management had always been skeptical of the traditional market research approaches in customer satisfaction measurement—skepticism rooted in the firm's long history of quantifying its operating standards. Its industrial engineers have gone so far as to determine how many steps it should take, on the average, for a driver to get from the truck to the front door.

Customer satisfaction is a different sort of phenomenon. It is subjective and intangible. But it can be measured objectively. Even though gauging the satisfaction of a customer is different from measuring how long it takes for a package to be delivered, accuracy of billing, the number of steps per driver, etc., for this company, it became clear early on that satisfaction too could be quantified with precision. Since customers' responses to survey questionnaires are noisy and often erratic, we stabilized its measures by combining the responses to several questions about overall satisfaction in such a way that the resulting measure was maximally related to repeat business. This can be done by linear programming or via statistical methods. We do the latter. Both the combining of responses and the calibration to repeat business are necessary in order to get a meaningful and forward-looking index of customer satisfaction. Without combining responses, there will be too much random noise in the measure. Without calibration to repeat business, the resulting measure will lack economic relevance.

In working with this company, we also learned quickly that it wasn't going to be helpful to ask customers what they considered important and then allocate resources accordingly. The problem was that it was difficult to get accurate and relevant responses. Even if management had good information on what their customers considered important, the usefulness of that information is limited. What's needed is information about the *impact* on customer satisfaction if the company changed something in the way it interacts with its customers. Customers are not always willing or able to reveal such information. We faced the additional problem that price was always mentioned by customers as extremely important and it was not clear how much of this was due to the customer-respondent as "negotiator" and how much was actual fact. When prices were increased, there was a temporary decline in customer satisfaction, but it wasn't permanent. Depending on the economic climate and competitive pricing, the effect on customer defection was usually small.

The concepts of "effect" and "marginal contributions" are critical here. Even though it may seem reasonable to do what customers say they want, it's not usually a wise strategy. One of the most fundamental tasks of any business is efficient allocation of resources. In a sense, this is what management decision making is all about. In this particular context, resources should be allocated based on the effects they have on customers—their satisfaction and retention—not on what may be important to them per se. For the shipping company, both price and service quality are important for customers, but a small change in quality has a much greater impact on customer satisfaction than a corresponding change in price. And the quality effect is more permanent.

The lessons? Focus on changes, not levels, Customers will not tell us what to do or how to run your business. Knowing the marginal contribution of a change is what's important—not what customers say is important. Price often has a direct and immediate effect on sales; it has a smaller long-term effect on customer satisfaction.

Another illustration of the difference between changes and levels comes from the Swedish Postal Service. This is an organization with a long-established culture of employee participation in management decisions. Just about everybody considered this to be highly important for the ability of the Swedish Postal Service to deliver reliable service to the public. Yet programs that allowed for increased participation had no effect, or, in some cases, an effect that was opposite to what was intended. Why? Because the level of employee participation was already at near-optimal. More was not needed.

The lesson? Because something is important to customers or employees doesn't mean that the organization should provide more of it. It's the impact that matters. And that's a different issue. But it's often not understood.

American Airlines paid a steep price for getting too close to its customers in reacting to what customers said they wanted. Like all the major U.S. air carriers in the late 1990s, American found itself under increasing pressure from various low-cost competitors. American's costs-per-mile for flying passengers were nearly twice that of Southwest Airlines, largely because of its fleet structure and labor contracts. Realizing that these costs made it difficult to compete on price, American decided on a differentiation strategy based on solving a long-standing gripe among air travelers, particularly among business "road warriors": the lack of legroom in coach class. By removing a couple of rows of seats, thus increasing the seat "pitch" (distance from a given point on one seat to the same point on the seat directly in front of or behind it) from the emerging industry standard of 31 to 33 inches, American provided a more spacious 34 or 35 inches.

When American announced its campaign, it made clear that the object was to increase revenue by filling more seats on its flights. As its pricing was already higher than its low-cost competitors, the airline would not seek to command a further premium for the increased passenger comfort. From the perspective of potential customers, American was offering genuine "added value" in an area of service that was widely considered a major source of passenger discontent.

Many took the news of American's plan as evidence of a newfound responsiveness to longstanding customer complaints. The business logic also seemed compelling. After all, why fly planes with rows of empty seats if you can capture additional market share and increase overall revenue simply by taking some of those seats out of the plane and filling the rest with "delighted" customers?

But by 2004 American had abandoned the "More Room Throughout Coach" program, refitting its planes back to the tighter seating configuration it had changed only four years earlier. The program became one of the most prominent and expensive marketing blunders in recent industry history. At first blush, it would be easy to attribute the demise of the program to the disasters that befell American between its initiation and conclusion. The combined shocks of the September 11 attacks (involving two American Airlines flights), the crash of American flight 587 shortly after takeoff in November of 2001, and public skittishness and fuel price instability made things difficult for all airlines.

But American stuck by the program for two years after the September 11 attacks, as the fundamental logic underlying the initiative seemed to still apply. Even as the industry's difficulties mounted, CEO Donald Carty claimed that "The More Room Throughout Coach Campaign . . . gained real traction in 2001, giving us an important point of differentiation versus the rest of the industry."[3]

Carty and American's management may have been right that 9/11 didn't change the appeal of the program, but that's not what's relevant. What *is* relevant is how extra legroom affects the satisfaction of the passenger. Even though most people, when asked, said that legroom was important to them, there was no significant effect on satisfaction. Legroom was not enough of a factor to override other considerations. Scheduling, loyalty programs and especially pricing remained the key drivers of travelers' choice of airlines, even to the detriment of their own comfort.

A BETTER WAY

Getting easily understood information in a timely manner is the backbone of Customer Asset Management operations. For companies with multiple retail outlets, this is of particular importance. It doesn't matter if we're talking about car dealers, stores, restaurants, bank branches, or fast-food outlets. Each unit manager needs a report from which action can be taken. The mathematics behind the numbers may be difficult, but that's true for many things and often has nothing to do with operations. It's not necessary to understand the machinery of a car in order to drive it. I may not know the workings of my television or my PC, but I know how to use them. The same is true for, say, the car dealership. The manager needs to know where the dealership stands on customer satisfaction and what should be done to improve it. In our Customer Asset Management Programs, we often communicate this in four categories: (1) What's wrong?; (2) What is likely to have caused it?; (3) What should be done about it?; and (4) How serious is the issue? For American Airlines, legroom would not be identified in the "what's wrong" category. Instead, we would have "lack of routes," scheduling problems, high cost, and other factors that have a strong impact on satisfaction. Here is an example of what it may look like.

What's wrong?

A significant number of your customers have reported problems with particular aspects of the warranty service they received at your car dealership. Specifically, your customers indicated that your service personnel lacked full understanding of their specific warranty service problem.

What caused it?

- Service Advisor(s) and/or technician(s) not sufficiently trained to properly diagnose and repair certain problems.
- Service Advisor(s) sufficiently trained, but does not listen with care to the customer's description of the problem.
- Service Advisor(s) does not carefully communicate the problem to the technician on the written Repair Order.
- Service advisor(s) does not follow up to assure that the technician properly repaired the problem.
- Customer is not capable of describing the problem properly to the Service Advisor(s).
- Service Adviser(s) does not communicate the complexity of the problem when taking the repair order or returning the car to the customer.

What should be done about it?

- Assure minimum competence of Service Advisors and technicians with appropriate hiring and training practices.
- Properly instruct and motivate Service Advisors to carefully question the customer and write down the problem in as much of the customer's language as possible.
- For certain problems areas, it is preferable to tell customer up front that there may be multiple causes which must be eliminated.
- Institute quality control system so that the car is not returned to customer until the Service Advisor verifies that the problem as described by the customer has been repaired.

How serious is the problem?

This particular problem calls for urgent attention, because taking no action will have major impact upon reducing your overall Customer Satisfaction. Action to correct this problem is very important.

STRATEGIC POSITIONING

There are two critical inputs to Customer Asset Management: (1) the impact or effect of different aspects of the product and the customer experience (such as customization, reliability, price, etc), and (2) the level of company performance, in the eyes of the customer, on these aspects, either in an absolute sense or relative to competitors.

| Low Impact & Strong Performance: Maintain or reduce investment or alter target market | High Impact & Strong Performance: Maintain or improve performance-Competitive advantage |
| Low Impact & Weak Performance: Inconsequential - Do not waste resources | High Impact & Weak Performance: Focus improvements here- Competitive vulnerability |

Figure 7.2   Customer Satisfaction Index

Source: American Customer Satisfaction Index

Weak performing attributes with high impact should be the first priority for improvement. For example, many companies perform poorly on service reliability, which often has a large impact on satisfaction. Product customization is another high impact area for many nondurable product manufacturers. But most competitors do well on this dimension such that even a small lead may reveal a competitive advantage leading to greater profits. When impact is low and performance weak, the data suggest that the customer neither demands nor is willing to pay for improvements, and efforts aimed at increasing satisfaction should be focused elsewhere. Finally, when impact is low and performance is strong, the data suggest that these qualities are taken for granted by the customer—they reflect a basic requirement for entry into the market— and that improvement efforts should be allocated to higher impact areas.

Strategically aligned companies are those that perform well in areas that have the greatest impact on customers, do not waste resources improving areas of little or no importance to customers, and get the basics right. Often there are important differences between high-performance and low-performance companies. Though both types of firms tend to perform more or less the same in low-impact areas, high-performance companies simply perform much better in high-impact areas.

The idea of strategic alignment can best be illustrated dynamically. Let's start with the disaster scenario. The starting point is a customer satisfaction matrix with "entries" in each quadrant. That is, there are attributes that have a high impact on customer satisfaction where we do well and there are attributes that have a high impact where we don't. Conversely, there are attributes with low impact—on some of these we do well, and on others we don't. The next matrix in the sequence illustrates the risk of adhering too closely to principles of Total Quality Management or Six Sigma, which calls for improvements in all weak areas. As suboptimal as this strategy is, it is still quite common in many companies, founded on the idea that whatever customers consider weak points or areas of underperformance, the firm needs to improve. However, such a strategy demands much more effort than is needed. It also leaves the firm vulnerable to customization attempts by competitors. In the disaster scenario, competitors become successful in shifting the salience of attributes that we do well on toward low impact. The end result is that in areas where we are strong, customers don't care and where we are weak, customers care a lot. No firm can survive under such circumstances.

By contrast, in a successful scenario, we would target low performing high-impact attributes for improvement and work to maintain superiority in high-impact areas where we are already performing well. As a result, the strategically aligned firm will expend far fewer resources on those attributes which, whether performing well or poorly, mean little to the satisfaction of its customers. Other attributes will be monitored, but as long as they have little impact, they warrant no action. The strategically aligned firm is optimizing the use of its resources by separating the relevant from the irrelevant and is much more likely to reap subsequent financial returns.

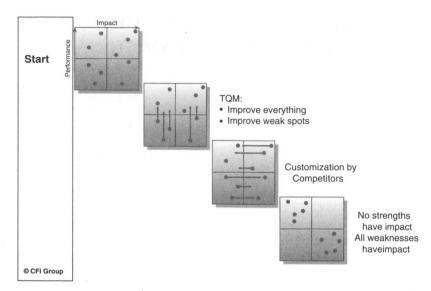

Figure 7.3 Disaster Sequence

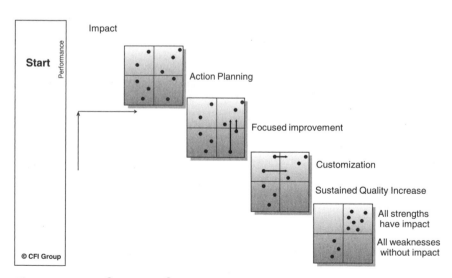

Figure 7.4 Success Sequence

GOOGLE—HIGH GROWTH, HIGH CUSTOMER SATISFACTION

Ever since e-business search engines were first included in the ACSI in 2002, Google has been a leader in customer satisfaction. What is Google doing right? Why does it have such a large and highly satisfied customer base? It's probably not that it is better at everything. It's more likely that it has done a good job picking its spots—areas that have a high impact on user satisfaction.

According to its users, Google's search engine produces results that are fast and accurate. Google prides itself on the speed with which search results are returned; there is a little window after each search that informs the user of precisely (to the 1/100 of a second) how long it took to get the results, a number usually under a quarter of a second. Not surprisingly, none of Google's major competitors is quite so transparent in advertising the speed of performance. Users also find that Google searches provide cleaner results with few or no "dead" pages or faulty links, saving time otherwise lost on pointless clicking. In short, Google provides a high performance product for its users. Second, Google has succeeded in being innovative without disrupting core functions. Over the last few years, it has been made possible to search specific categories of information—scholarly articles, online books, content with images, and local news and information, but the web page has remained basic and familiar to most users.

Third, Google has built on its strengths and resources to find additional sources of revenue, but again without losing sight of its core business. For instance, the company has expanded business by licensing technology to companies and universities for using Google technology for internal searches. Whether users are aware of it or not, many of the search functions performed on these intranets use Google. A source of considerable profit has been the methods used for integrating advertising into the search functions and returning sponsored links related to the search. This is an example of matching buyers to sellers and, if done well, is probably the most potent contributor to customer satisfaction.

The number of unique visitors to Google has surpassed Microsoft but lags behind Yahoo, a company that has faced management and strategy challenges but seems to have corrected course with customer with a big 2007 upswing in ACSI. The combination of high levels of customer satisfaction and the offering of a strong nonrival product is the key factor for explosive growth. Google has created tremendous value for its investors, but it is difficult to see how such growth can continue, regardless of how high customer satisfaction may go.

eBay is another interesting example of a company with strong customer satisfaction, but it doesn't have quite the same degree of nonrival offerings as Google does. To the extent that its electronic auctions are limited by physical goods whose consumption cannot be shared, eBay's growth is, by definition, limited. My search on Google does not impede anybody else's search, but my purchase of a car on eBay makes it impossible for someone else to buy the same car. But if you offer all sellers and all buyers around the world to interact with one another—which is close to what eBay does—this type of growth limitation may not matter much. Among electronic retailers, eBay has consistently been at the top in customer satisfaction, with a large lead over uBid and Priceline.com. It has fared nearly as well as overall satisfaction leaders, Amazon and Barnesandnoble.com. eBay does far more than serve as an auction site and now sells both new and used products in almost 50,000 distinct categories. With over 230 million registered users, up from just 22 million in 2000, eBay has seen its revenue increase by nearly 1300 percent in less than a decade. The company has also greatly expanded its services and broken into new markets—both within the United States and internationally—through acquisitions and strategic partnerships. So what is the secret to eBay's success?

eBay's customer satisfaction success lies in the matching principle— the most powerful builder of a strong customer asset base. In many ways, the company has developed a mastery of mass customization.

Mass customization is about producing goods and/or services that meet different *individual* customer's needs with the efficiency of mass *production*. It is highly dependent on information, and very few companies have succeeded as well as eBay. The process of making a transaction on the eBay website is simple and designed to treat each customer as a unique individual. The website's home page is headed with a search function in which the user enters the name of the product sought. Specific search terms yield specific search results, taking users where they want to go, while less specific search terms bring up a group of "best matching" subcategories to help narrowing the search. Once a product has been located, purchasing is done through a competitive bidding process, and payment is made (typically) through the eBay-owned Pay Pal service, which validates credit cards and protects both buyer and seller from fraud.

Because eBay brings buyers and sellers together from locations anywhere in the world, most people can find just about anything they may be looking for. How about Pope Benedict XVI's car, a man from Arizona's air guitar, and clippings from Britney Spear's shaved head (although the latter was later suspended)?

eBay and Google are similar in that both companies saw opportunity in a new technology for creating a service that was previously unavailable in the way we now think about it. In 2005, Google had an ACSI score of 82 (well above the national average of about 74) and had created shareholder wealth to the tune of about $100 billion. Perhaps not quite as spectacular, eBay has done all right with an ACSI score of 81 and about $44 billion of shareholder wealth creation.

But eBay and Google are not unique in creating shareholder satisfaction (which one would assume follows wealth) via, at least in part, high customer satisfaction. Consider what the following companies have in common: General Electric, Procter & Gamble, Coca-Cola, United Parcel Service, PepsiCo, Apple, Wachovia, and Lowe's. Some make soft drinks, others ship packages; some have thousands of brick-and-mortar locations; others are durable goods manufacturers. The group elder, Procter & Gamble, was founded in 1837—the year Queen Victoria ascended the throne of the United Kingdom, Michigan became a state, and a year after the Battle of the Alamo. 158 years later, eBay got its start—the year something called a "DVD player" was first introduced.

Before we connect these companies, how about these: AT&T, AOL Time Warner, Albertsons, Qwest Communications, Reliant Energy, NiSource, Xcel Energy, Charter Communications, US Airways, and Safeway? Do they have anything in common? They too offer very different goods and services, compete in different sectors of the economy, and run the gamut as to origins and longevity in business.

Here's the thread that binds all of them together: The first group has created wealth for its shareholders. The second group has destroyed wealth. The first group has also created satisfied customers; the second group has not. It is also noteworthy how much better the companies in the first group have been in producing satisfied customers. Their average ACSI score is 81. The corresponding average for the second group is 67.

This is consistent with the findings from the analysis of stock prices and customer satisfaction. High customer satisfaction and shareholder wealth tend to go together. The companies in the high satisfaction group

Table 7.1 High and Low MVA/ACSI Companies*

Company	ACSI	MVA (in $billions)
High ACSI-High MVA Companies		
General Electric Company	81	282,545.2
The Procter & Gamble Company	82	172,733.9
Google Inc.	82	103,763.7
The Coca Cola Company	84	83,943.7
United Parcel Service of America, Inc.	82	66,396.8
PepsiCo, Inc.	82	65,024.3
Apple Computer, Inc.	81	43,832.1
e-Bay, Inc.	81	43,585.6
Wachovia Corporation	79	41,914.4
Lowe's Companies, Inc.	78	33,647.1
Average	**81**	**93,738.7**
Sum		**937,386.9**

Continued

Table 7.1 Continued

Low ACSI-Low MVA Companies

AT&T Corporation	72	−29,393.3
AOL Time Warner Inc	71	−23,194.5
Albertsons, Inc.	71	−6,624.8
Qwest Communications (US WEST)	69	−3,973.0
Reliant Energry	69	−1,795.7
NiSource, Inc. (Nipsco Industries)	68	−459.4
Xcel	68	−175.3
Charter Communications	56	44.1
USAir Group, Inc.	57	896.7
Safeway, Inc.	71	922.4
Average	**67**	**−6,375.3**
Sum		**−63,752.8**

Source: American Customer Satisfaction Index; MVA from Stern Stewart & Co.

generated close to $1 trillion for their shareholders. The companies in the low satisfaction group destroyed a little more than $60 billion. Almost 50 percent of that was due to AT&T, which suffered both eroding customer satisfaction and MVA during a period of heavy merger and acquisition activity. Perhaps things will change as the company's leadership has changed. Randall Stephenson, the new Chairman and CEO, is not planning to make additional acquisitions but rather to increase the satisfaction of AT&T's customers by adding many more services and putting wireless at the forefront of the new AT&T. Market Value Added (MVA) measures the difference between what investors have put in and what they can take out of a company. It is equal to market value minus all capital from equity and debt offerings, loans, retained earnings, and capitalization of R&D spending. A positive MVA implies that the firm has created a positive return to its shareholders. A firm with negative MVA has destroyed shareholder wealth.[4]

Is this true in general? Have companies with high customer satisfaction also done better for their shareholders? The answer is yes, they have done a lot better. Looking at the most recent year of available data (2006), the top 25 percent of firms in the ACSI boast an average MVA of $44.1 billion, while those in the bottom 25 percent

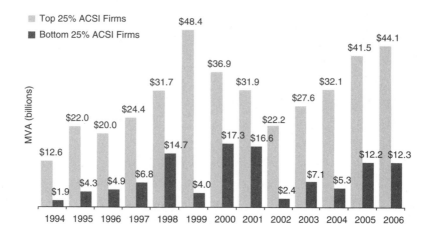

Figure 7.5 Average Market Value Added: High and Low ACSI Firms*

*Source: MVA from Stem Stewart & Co.; Annually Updated ACSI Firms

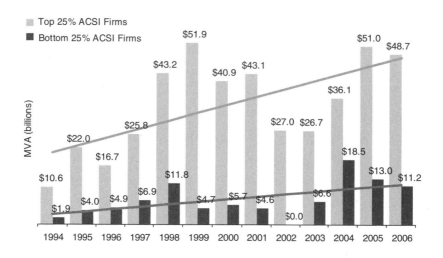

Figure 7.6 Average Market Value Added: Over Time*

*Source: MVA from Stem Stewart & Co.; Baseline 1994 ACSI Firms only

average $12.3 billion. That's some difference! What's more, every single year, the high customer satisfaction companies do better—usually much better.

In order to get an idea of how customer satisfaction and MVA move together over time, we need to look at the same firms over time. That's what figure 7.6 shows. Not only do high customer satisfaction firms have higher levels of MVA, they also seem to grow their market value added at a faster rate—not each and every year, but the trend is apparent.

The story is different for airlines in the United States: Unhappy passengers and unhappy investors. For the established carriers, business has been challenging. Security issues, cost of fuel, labor problems, crowded airspace, and airports are some of the problems. But management has probably contributed to the problems. Poor communications, bad service, and cost cutting in the wrong places have exacerbated the situation. The airlines are among the lowest scoring companies in customer satisfaction. Investors haven't been pleased either. But the airline business is not completely different from most other businesses. It can be good for passengers and investors alike. That's been proven by Southwest Airlines in the United States and Ryanair in Europe. Both have done well by following a different business model compared with the other more established carriers. Both airlines are no frills discounters with much lower fixed costs than the traditional airlines. Compared with its competition, Southwest provides much higher passenger satisfaction and has created much greater shareholder value.

Charter Communications hasn't done much for shareholders or customers. With an ACSI score of 56, Charter ranked as low as or worse than any private sector company measured in 2005. Its MVA was $44 million—not much for a company with 6 million customers, 17,000 employees, and more than $5 billion in revenue (in 2006). For comparison, the largest 500 companies in the United States have an MVA average of $15 billion.

The reason that some firms do well and others poorly has much less to do with the industry they happen to compete in than it does with how they are managed. Winners are separated from losers by how they manage customer assets. I am not sure that there is another area of management that is more important but stuffed with so many faulty assumptions, inaccurate data, and counterproductive strategy. What is clear is that barriers to switching are coming down and customer satisfaction is becoming even more critical for financial success. But it often takes time to create a satisfied customer. It may take even longer to be rewarded for it. It requires strength to withstand a narrow cost-focus orientation and too parochial a view of productivity as a primary driver of company performance. The problem for companies with low levels of customer satisfaction is that they are forced to compete on price—whether or not they have cost structure or efficiencies to do it well. Even in a growth economy, it pays to devote more attention to the management of the current customer base. In low growth or in saturated markets, the customer asset is even more critical. How can it best be protected from competition? After all, it is the origin of the dominant part of revenue and profit for most firms. In general, something like 80 percent of total revenue comes from current customers. Most repeat business is dependent on how satisfied the customers are. Satisfaction, in turn, depends on how well the company's products and services are customized to the buyer, their quality, and their price. In that order. The dividends from repeat business from a satisfied customer are sizeable. There are exceptions to this rule, but they are not many. Keeping customers by price concessions is a losing battle. Not only is it expensive, but it does not lead to strong customer relationships. Getting close to your customers is a good idea—but not too close. Customers negotiate. Customers are difficult. Customers demand more for less. A customer-centric company doesn't let its customers run the business.

The intelligent company doesn't always do what customers say they want. It finds the intersection between customer satisfaction and profitability and invests its resources for the best marginal return on both. It does not waste resources on improving things that its customers may want but are not willing to pay for.

CHAPTER 8

Putting the Numbers to Work

Having lived and worked in many places around the globe, I know at once both its vastness as well as its tendency to make small-world connections when you don't expect it. And so one day after presenting a seminar in Minneapolis, Minnesota, on the importance of customer experience, a young woman approached me saying that a mutual friend had recommended that we connect for a cup of coffee. Little did I know at the time the importance that meeting would have. From my early days of training as a cryptologist in the Swedish intelligence and throughout my career as a researcher, numbers and quantification have always been important. But to have impact, to change things (presumably for the better), the numbers must be put to work. At CFI, we sometimes say that we supply the best numbers money can buy. I think that's true, but the value of numbers dissipates quickly unless they are used correctly. And putting them to use requires a lot of hard work, especially when dealing with large organizations where people have vastly different backgrounds and responsibilities.

Enter Julie Beth McFall, the head of Best Buy's Customer Experience Research Team. Julie Beth and her team were responsible for a dramatic transformation of Best Buy's approach to managing the customer experience. At the time, they were looking to partner with somebody who could help develop a better way for gaining insights into Best Buy's customer interactions and using those insights to strengthen customer relationships. We sat down in the sunny atrium of the hotel where I was giving the seminar and got to know a little about each other. Julie Beth had joined Best Buy some five years earlier after receiving her Ph.D. at Indiana University's Kelley School of Business and serving on the faculty of the Carlson School of Management at the University of Minnesota. Her expertise was in the fields of organizational behavior and international business. Organizational behavior, in particular, came in handy at Best Buy—a large retailer of consumer electronics, home office products, software, and appliances with over 800 stores in the United States.

We talked about people we both knew and she told me about her move from academia to business; how she wanted to take advantage of systems theory in real applications—not just teach and do research. Best Buy had offered her a significant role in what was going to be a major organizational transformation that she had taught her students about: management, rewards, structure, leadership, motivation, and how to best mix job responsibilities with private life. Now she was faced with the challenge of making Best Buy a truly customer-oriented organization. Not that the company had been a stranger to the idea that it had to compete for the satisfaction of its customers; in fact, much of its earlier success could be traced to it.

Best Buy was founded as Sound of Music in 1966 by Dick Schulz, who triple mortgaged his house to start the company. The first year ended with $173,000 in gross sales. Three years later, Sound of Music's annual sales reached $1 million. An inkling of what was to be came in 1981, when a tornado ripped through one of the stores. After retrieving the inventory, the company held a huge merchandise sale, which turned out to be a big success. Soon thereafter, the stores reached $350 in sales per square foot; almost doubled the industry average. Prices were low and customers received good value for the money.

In 1983, Sound of Music changed its name to Best Buy to better fit the new marketing strategy and because it would be listed ahead of competition in the phone book. "We won't be undersold on any items," became the mantra. In 1985, Best Buy offered 650,000 shares of stock on NASDAQ and raised $8 million. An additional offering in 1986 raised $33.6 million, which helped finance a 12-store expansion. Best Buy continued to grow and debuted on NYSE in 1987. Stores entered Texas and Chicago in 1991, and Best Buy became the first national retailer of both DVD hardware and software in 1997, began selling HDTV in 1998, acquired Magnolia Hi Fi in 2000, added Canada's Future Shop and U.S.-based Musicland in 2001, and opened the first global sourcing office in Shanghai in 2003. When *Forbes* Magazine named Best Buy "Company of the Year" in 2004, sales were growing rapidly and in 2006, revenue passed $40 billion.

I shared some of my own background and experience working with large companies, some of them retailers, with Julie Beth. I described the Customer Asset Management approach of CFI. I think that both of us saw a similar vision of something exciting and truly important. The timing was fortuitous because Best Buy had all but concluded its search for a vendor partner when we met. At the 11th hour, CFI made its case for why our approach would be the right one for their transformation, and the partnership was sealed.

THE JOURNEY BEGINS

When Julie Beth became director of Customer Experience Research for Best Buy, she inherited a customer satisfaction program that had been in place for a few years and had gone through two or three iterations over the years. The problem was that it wasn't used to its full potential. It was similar to a situation with her new house, she said. Shortly before she began the Best Buy transformation journey, she bought a new house. Among the features of this house was a rather elaborate security system, completed with flashing lights and bells that went off each time a door was opened or closed. A day or so after taking possession, she called the former owner to inquire about the security code and the billing for this system. The former owner laughed and said that it wasn't actually connected to anything—it looked good, had lots of bells and whistles, and it even had a security sign in the yard, but it didn't alert the police or fire department. Just in case the wrong people read this, Julie Beth tells me that a new and connected system has since been installed. Though not totally disconnected to operations, the previous customer satisfaction program at Best Buy was not unlike the security system. More than 700 Best Buy stores received daily reports, replete with numbers, data, and rankings, reflecting feedback from many thousands of customers. However, in most cases, store managers were left holding sheets of paper, wondering what to do with them. Not only did they not provide customer insights, but—like the security system—they didn't actually connect to other key metrics in the organization, and they didn't show managers what to do with the information. When comparing the deluge of daily data to financial and operational performance metrics, it wasn't clear that anything was really related. The reports were of no help for stores to focus their energies on improving customer service and, above all, they had no predictive power. But they did have the bells and whistles of a detailed customer satisfaction program.

When I first met with Julie Beth, one of the topics about which she was most passionate was the linkages between what customers tell us via surveys, written comments, and phone calls, and key operational metrics such as traffic, turnover, and store financial performance. Given that this was something I had done many times using the CFI methodology, I was certain that we could help her do this at Best Buy.

"Gone are the days when our customer loyalty or satisfaction scores are trending down while company growth is trending up!" she said with a smile.

I was hoping that we wouldn't let her down. My thinking on systems and connectivity had evolved over many years of combined teaching, research, forming my own companies, and helping other companies manage their customer assets. I had come to the conclusion that it made sense to look at everybody as an investor. The company invests in customer assets. The customer invests in seller relationships. The employee invests in the working environment of the company. The key to making all investors work together in a mutually beneficial manner would be to make sure that risks are low enough and that the returns are high enough for all participants. Clearly, teaching the Best Buy work force to use the information and to leverage it for a better understanding of how customer experience is related to key metrics was important. It would make Best Buy a better company for customers, employees, and shareholders.

Julie Beth and her team set out to build a program platform based on four key components. First, the output from the feedback mechanism had to tie to key financial, operational, and human talent metrics. It would be of little value to know the drivers of customer satisfaction unless they could be linked to internal processes and operations on the one hand and to financial results on the other. Second, the output had to be easy to understand. Third, it had to be actionable—helping store managers to improve customer satisfaction at the local level. And fourth, it had to help stores build better relationships with customers by understanding individual differences as well as overarching needs and desires. Instead of focusing on a purely transactional basis, the platform sought to understand cumulative experiences, engagement, and predict future customer behavior. A tall order!

Julie Beth knew that her team couldn't build a new platform like this on its own. Their first step was to hit the road crisscrossing the country in order to get Best Buy's vast retail field organization on board. The team held co-creation groups in many cities around the United States with Best Buy associates and managers discussing what would be most meaningful, useful, and helpful in driving engagement and a better customer experience. From these discussions, Julie Beth and her team were able to put together a plan that met the needs of all parties—and thereby gained the buy-in of the individuals who would eventually use the information each and every workday. In the end, they even had the retail guys participate in a contest to name the new program—they now took even more ownership of it.

CREATING A NEW CULTURE

Anytime you have an almost 40-year-old company, there's a long history of anecdotes that create a powerful culture. Best Buy has many of these—stories about the founder mortgaging his home to start Sound of Music, stories about the massive tornado that almost closed the company for good but led instead to the "tornado sale" that rallied the employees toward a better future. With deeply held beliefs about how the organization does business, thinks about customers, and uses data, introducing massive changes was not going to be an easy task. Clearly, we all had our work cut out for us. Among other things, there was a shift in terminology. How customer experience is measured, reported, calculated, "score carded," and understood—all of these were changing. But even more importantly, the philosophical approach to managing *relationships* instead of *transactions* was an even bigger change. Organic growth in the sense that it was to come from the existing customers was the name of the game. With the runway of new customers getting smaller, building relationships with existing customers was paramount.

In a retail setting where abundance exists, products are commoditizing faster and faster and where access to alternatives is a mouse click away, growth is vital. Driving more customers through the door is one thing, but differentiation is what really matters. Think about the United States as a marketplace, with hundreds of millions of consumers. It might seem reasonable to believe that there is a never-ending supply of *new* customers available to spend their disposable income in our stores or online. However, when we peel back the layers of customer availability, what we find is that most of them have already shopped in one of Best Buy's stores and they may or may not come back. If they had a bad experience, why would they come back for more? Better to make sure, to the extent possible, that Best Buy's customers had a good experience and that they were highly satisfied with the products they bought. Add to the dwindling pool of new customers those whose income precludes discretionary spending on the kinds of items Best Buy sells and those too young to afford most electronics products, and the pool of brand new, never-before-shopped-at-Best-Buy, customers becomes even smaller. This means that each existing customer is getting more important—each customer interaction, or "moment of truth" matters more.

Service channels provide a great opportunity for differentiation via "relationship building" because interactions at this level are quite personal. A customer who invites a Geek Squad agent (Best Buy's home service technicians) into his or her home to work on a personal computer is taking the transactional level experience to another level. Just think how important your own computer is to your daily life, and think about the person who recovers your precious data or makes it possible for you to surf the Internet at the speed of light. There are Best Buy stories about Geek Squad agents who have been so warmly received after an appointment that they have been invited to join the family for dinner. When a Home Theater installation agent spends several hours in a customer's family room setting up the perfect home theater, the agent becomes a hero as the home just turned into the place where everyone wanted to watch the Super Bowl!

One of the challenges the team at Best Buy faced was creating new language around customers and building "customer experience" into the DNA of the organization. It began at the top of "the house" with a leadership team, passionate about the importance of the customer experience to the ultimate well-being of the company and its employees. Feedback from customers were made available to everyone in the company through a common portal. The language was woven into conversations; team after team was trained on the platform—what it could tell them and how to get to the data. Customer experience and customer health even became a permanent topic at board of directors meetings. The insights were being sought after by people at all levels of the organization. As information was made available, everyone from Brad Anderson, president of Best Buy, to the analysts, had their eye on the new platform. According to Julie Beth, the best part of the process was that people believed that they were learning something important that would help them focus on what was most important to their customers.

HOLISTIC APPROACH

One of the examples Julie Beth shared with me early on was that of a customer who had been considering buying a new laptop for some time. After thinking about it for a few months, he decided to log into the bestbuy.com website to do some research. Once he had narrowed his choices down to two potential alternatives based on price and features, he went into his local Best Buy store. He spent some time with a computer sales specialist discussing the pros and cons of each, and finally made a choice and purchased his laptop. At that point, he went home and called the 1–800 BestBuy number to make an appointment to have one of the Geek Squad agents come to his home to set up the computer with software and install a wireless network. A couple of days later, a Geek Squad agent arrived at his house and installed the desired software and set up his wireless network.

While all of this seems simple enough on the surface, the problem was that at no point other than at the in-store point of sale did Best Buy formally seek feedback from the customer, and at no point in the process did any of these different channels (online, in the store, on the phone, and in the home) "talk" with one another or connect insights with one another. To Best Buy, it was as though the customer had dealt with four different companies and as if the company had dealt with four separate customers. Yet, there was only one customer, and, from the customers' perspective, there was only one company.

Thus the glaring need—if Best Buy truly wanted to build relationships and understand the complete customer experience—was to start connecting the various points of contact and to solicit feedback from customers at more than one point in the process. So while the retail platform was being built, so was a multi-faceted online experience assessment, as well as a service (e.g., installation) component. Within the halls of Best Buy, new conversations began taking place—conversations between Julie Beth's team and the BestBuy.com research team, between Julie Beth's team and the leaders of the phone channel, between her team and the various services teams, and between her team and the human talent teams responsible for employee engagement. A lot of teams. A lot of work. And a lot of synergy that hadn't been there before. New questions were asked:

- How do experiences across these channels relate to one another?
- How does an experience in one channel affect experiences or opinions across channels?
- Where are the pain points?
- Where are the breakdowns?
- Where are we providing end to end solutions well?
- What is the role of engaged employees in driving a better customer experience?
- What are we learning in each channel that can be leveraged to understand the holistic customer experience?

Internally even more was done. While putting feedback mechanisms in place throughout every channel in the company was a start, being diligent about bringing these perspectives and insights together was necessary for the next step. So Best Buy created a council of key researchers who all had insights and access to customer data—through surveys, databases, transactional information, etc.—and they started the first truly holistic conversations. This council looked for common themes, issues, wins, problems, pain points, "dissatisfiers," and opportunities, and recommended to management where to put resources to enhance customer satisfaction.

REALLY LISTENING

As discussed previously, the customer with a complaint that we never hear may well be our biggest problem. Each of these customers represents not only lost revenue and profits in the future, but also reflects a failure in communication with costly consequences. The lessons lost by not knowing what went wrong are equally valuable. And, perhaps worst of all, the dissatisfied, frustrated, former customer may become an impassioned anti-advocate of our company—spreading negatives to other current or potential customers. One of the ways Best Buy is trying to remedy the frustrations of dissatisfied customers is by encouraging them to voice their concerns and have someone in the organization designated to resolve them. As part of the focus on customer experience, Best Buy had its new customer experience platform include a program through which customers who completed a retail- or services-related survey and indicated low overall satisfaction or mentioned an unresolved problem could request a follow-up contact from either the store general manager or services manager. In the pilot phase alone, thousands of customers requested this call back and the results were astounding. Going from pilot to a national program in over 800 stores was never in question. Every store had to have this program. It was launched with strong support from the general managers who took local accountability for repairing broken relationships with disenchanted customers.

To think that a big box retailer actually cared enough to call or write to an individual customer apparently blew some customers away. In many cases, people just wanted to vent or voice a concern, and often a sincere apology or effort to remedy a bad situation personally went a long way. While this turned out to be an important lesson in local accountability and repairing relationships, it also translated into a tool for learning how to prevent future problems. By understanding firsthand what Best Buy was doing wrong, managers learned how to coach and train employees to prevent the same problems from occurring again, and to solve the problems before they escalate. Differentiation?

You bet. Accountability? Building relationships? Yep. Encouraging feedback on problems? Absolutely. And, these things made a difference. The stores that were involved in the pilot program saw better scores in the areas of problem resolution and overall satisfaction than those not in the pilot.

Learning from the quantitative data gathered through surveys provides one lens on customer experience. Another one comes from the calls and written comments that customers provide in addition to the surveys. Thousands of customers take the time to call in or write their personal experience on the surveys, to tell the name of their sales person, the items that were and were not in stock, or the unique challenges they faced. Ensuring that these comments make their way to where they matter most (e.g., store, service channel) and that they are read and used as a source of insight is essential. While listening to customers and learning about how well we are delivering on the overall experience is important for making immediate changes, we also know the importance of looking out into the future. In keeping with the buyer utility concept, it is critical to understand how a customer experiences in the present can serve as an indication of future behavior.

For Best Buy, one way to do this was to take today's customer satisfaction scores at the individual level and then track behavior of individual customers over the ensuing months. Not surprisingly, the team found that those customers with high satisfaction scores also scored higher on self-ratings of future behavior such as recommending Best Buy or returning to purchase another item. And they also spent more money in the months following their survey response compared to those customers who had lower customer satisfaction scores.

During the retail co-creation groups the year before, Best Buy implemented the new customer experience platform, and the customer experience research team captured useful commentary from general managers as well as from store associates. At the time of the transformation, stores received daily downloads of customer data—literally pages of numbers and rankings and percentages. However, managers were at a loss as to where to begin making improvements. One general manager commented "Sure, I got four pages of data, but you know what I look at? I read the top one inch. I look at the overall satisfaction percentage and the ranking. After that, it's anyone's guess as to where to put our efforts." This struck a strong chord with Julie Beth's team. They knew that they had to provide insights and data that helped managers focus energy and address such concerns as:

- What has the biggest impact on satisfaction?
- What should the store work on first?
- What is different in one store than another?
- Where are stores already doing well?

AVOIDING THE GAMING GAME

How do you take a program rich with insight and information about the customer experience and encourage everyone to use it without rewarding them directly for doing so? True, if you tie customer satisfaction metrics to pay bonuses, it's likely that the metrics will get a lot of attention. If the metrics are unreliable or inaccurate, there is an obvious problem. But there is another issue that is equally serious which occurs when numbers can be changed without an underlying change in what they are supposed to reflect. Gaming of the system is a serious problem in many companies. This occurs in all stages from collection of data through computation. I have seen employees fill out customer surveys and sales people pressuring customers to give them high marks. When this happens, the metrics aren't real and the numbers can't be put to work.

The year that the new customer experience platform was launched at Best Buy, each week the research team received multiple e-mails and calls from managers asking for "the metric" that should be used on everyone's performance appraisal. After all, they would say, "If we are a customer centric company that cares about the customer experience, then we *must* have a customer metric tied to people's pay!" This became one of the greatest challenges. How to rally a company that for 40 years had been devoted to scorecards, rankings, and benchmarks related to a company objective and now not tie the new direction directly to pay? How to teach people to care about something when their pay was not directly (or so it seemed) affected by it? How to show that it mattered most but not put it on the all-important scorecard?

There were three parts addressing this issue. First was the "communication and visibility" plan. Then, the "behaviors and linkages" plan. And third, the "give it time" plan. Together these ideas allowed the company to work toward having a consistent emphasis on customer feedback without setting specific performance targets about it. The "communication and visibility" plan was the process by which the new platform was introduced, rolled-out, and shared with the organization at-large. There were team meetings, presentations, kick-offs, articles, and employee teams across the country that took shared responsibility for the launch. Senior executives visited stores, asked questions about what managers were learning about the customer experience via the new tool, and held them accountable for being aware of and for understanding what customers were telling them. The "behaviors and linkages" part of the plan was about promoting the "right behaviors" instead of the "right numbers"—behaviors such as how frequently customer feedback was incorporated into strategies and action plans, how well-versed managers were leveraging the insights from the customer feedback, how often it was used for coaching or recognition, and how it was used in communications with the in-store staff. As the services channels also geared up with their respective versions of the retail program, they too were challenged to articulate what they were doing differently based on the feedback. This was very different to what Best Buy was used to. This was not about driving performance to some magic number. As the first year drew to an end, we were able to begin establishing linkages between top performing stores and key financial and operational metrics. By sharing this information across the organization, the platform took on more credibility and importance as a means by which created a better experience for customers that then translated into business growth and financial returns.

As more and more customer feedback was collected with the new tools and processes, it was compared with the other metrics the company deemed important. Through this process, relationships started to emerge. As one metric rose, so did another. The stores that were top performers in operational or financial metrics were far and away the best in the customer metrics. There was simply no way for this data to be ignored if one wanted a more complete picture of the Best Buy business. The second year was about taking that a step further and creating predictive models that helped demonstrate the downstream benefits of today's improvements in customer satisfaction.

And, finally, the "give it time" part of the plan, the pinch hitter. Purely from a logistics standpoint, with no baseline data from previous years, no comparable scores from another time period or measurement device, and no experience from observing trends or seasonal changes, it was not feasible to set constructive targets. Here too many companies go wrong. Targets are important, but without sufficient information about where to set them, it's better not to have them until they can be determined with purpose and knowledge. So the team bought time—enough such that within that first year or two, they would, instead, get it right: Teach about service behaviors and useful ways to think about customer feedback and what it could do for the organization. In the end, everyone from the field to corporate staff asked about and sought information from the database in order to shape how they thought about their work. By removing the pressure to meet a specific number, Best Buy wanted to find out just how the customer feedback metrics were used, how they were incorporated into strategic plans, how many times stores were leveraging the data portal per week, how many customer problems were solved (or how many fewer there were), and so on. I am not sure it was like being freed from the tyranny of numbers but that's what I was told. . Since there was no direct link between staff or managerial compensation to the new metrics, any incentive to "game the system" was greatly diminished. All the energy that would have been spent trying to figure out how to get high scores were now directed toward the actual task of listening and serving the customer. Objectives and targets are important and often necessary. Relating targets to compensation can be a food motivator. But it is even better, albeit more difficult, to relate targets to the substantive behavior and efforts of the relevant individuals.

HITTING THE ROAD

How can you build a tool for someone without knowing what they want or need? Although we could sit around all day and poke holes in Best Buy's existing customer feedback platform, we couldn't possibly know all the intricacies of trying to use it every day, or what would make it better and more useful for the people dealing with customers on a day-to-day basis. Unless, we asked. So we did. We worked with Julie Beth's team to develop a "co-created" presentation (co-creating ideas with end users was new and very in vogue at the time at Best Buy). Her team went from city to city meeting in district offices with dozens upon dozens of Best Buy employees. The main purpose of the meetings was to listen. The idea was to let the employees tell the team what would be most meaningful. Reporting interfaces, reporting frequencies, and how to build a tool that was easier for customers to use (e.g., a survey that takes 7 minutes versus 23 minutes) were discussed. The prospective end users talked about the kinds of things they would expect customer feedback to link back to. They suggested what the most important questions were to ask customers. According to Julie Beth, "We listened—really let them drive, and then we came back to Minneapolis with videos and flip charts and notes, and went to work creating a more powerful tool.

"Right then we knew what one of our biggest opportunities was," Julie Beth continued. "Make it user-friendly, simple, meaningful, and facilitate getting the store employees focused on what was important—not being bogged down in data dumps."

NEW LANGUAGE

For the past six years, the customer measurement program at Best Buy was known as the "Loyalty" program. This term had been used by a hundred thousand employees in stores across the country. It had become engrained in the language of goals and leadership. But, "Loyalty" took on a new definition with the launch of the Reward Zone program, the new customer loyalty platform. During the design and development of the new customer experience platform, all store employees had been invited to suggest a name for the program. The Reward Zone was the winning suggestion, but even with a snappy new name the work to change how employees would think about and talk about the customer experience was just beginning. First, the name had to be communicated. That meant establishing credibility of the platform and its role in providing information about customer relationships in a very operational manner. Employees also needed to be educated about why the new program was better and different than the old one. Part of the problem was that the old program was very familiar to most, but it wasn't considered instrumental or effective in understanding the customer experience or in growing the business. A case for change had to be built by making a compelling argument for change. Enlisting help from the end users in the field gave the credibility needed. Without having had these people involved in the construction of the Reward Zone program, it might have been dead in the water.

A lot was promised—linkages, insights, action ability, ease of use—even before the field leadership had used the new tools. It was interesting to see how Julie Beth and her colleagues began to slowly but surely use words like "customer experience" and "customer health" and, ultimately, a customized ACSI measure fully replaced the old "Loyalty" program. But it took time and it took effort. Julie Beth's team trained, explained, and drove the case for change throughout the organization. They jokingly threatened to fine people $50 each time they said "Loyalty" instead of "True Blue" (the color of the University of Michigan) or customer experience. There were training sessions, presentations, web linkages, store signage, communications in internal publications, and promotions of the new name, concept, value, and benefits to everyone who would listen. I have worked with many organizations, but this was one of the most impressive and doggedly persistent attempts to really change an organization that I can remember. Changing language that is so deeply embedded in the organization takes time and tremendous effort. But one year after its initial launch, employees of Best Buy do in fact speak a new language. But the journey was not without bumps. About seven months into the new program, after a lot of hard work and when Julie Beth thought that it wasn't possible to do more in terms of promotion and communication, she received a phone call from the corporate office about revising employee orientation materials. They were planning to include some material around "Loyalty," but thought it might be good just to check with Julie Beth to make sure that the materials hadn't changed. Her first thought was "thank goodness he called!" Her second thought was "how long is this going to take!?" Now, we know. It took a little more than a year.

To further cement the new program, Best Buy set up a group that meets on a regular basis with the purpose of identifying current "points-of-pain" and priorities. It prepares a report that is shared with the rest of the organization. The "owners" of the issues are responsible for addressing the areas that are causing the most customer dissatisfaction. This is never easy. But, focusing energy on the things that matter is a place to start. Think back to the individual I described earlier as purchasing a laptop and actually touching every possible channel, from the initial research on the web to the final installation. If we knew where in the process things were most susceptible to breakdowns, we could take corrective action before any damage is done and achieve seamless service from start to finish. And, in a competitive service-oriented world, where the cost of time is rising, this is what matters.

Even though Best Buy has come a long way in a relatively short period of time, the company is still only in the beginning of a journey that will never end. It's been interesting to see how some of the most difficult problems have been tackled; How managers and associates have changed from looking at customer loyalty as an important objective to an understanding of the forces that lead to profitable repeat business; And the strength to resist calls for quantitative targets when there wasn't any basis for determining what they should be. As both Julie Beth and I had anticipated, we found a strong relationship between purchase behavior and customer satisfaction. Satisfied customers buy more and come back more frequently. As Best Buy creates more satisfied customers, profits will increase. That doesn't mean that Best Buy, or any other company for that matter, is immune to general market forces. They have some degree of protection, but not immunity. When the new customer experience program had been in effect for a while and was getting more traction, Best Buy's quarterly earnings fell by 18 percent. But customer satisfaction was getting stronger. What happened?

As far as I could determine, the positive relationship between customer satisfaction and earnings still held. But, as always, things have to be put in context. Yes, earnings were down, but revenue was up. Best Buy sold $1 billion worth of goods more than the year before. Same-store sales were up as well. So too was market share. But earnings were hurt by low margins in the newly opened business in China. That's not particularly surprising. But even more telling was what happened to Best Buy's major competitor. For the same quarter, the first in 2007, Circuit City reported a loss of $55 million. Revenue fell as well. Same-store sales slipped. Customer satisfaction dropped. Accordingly, the pattern that we have observed so often remained intact. The strength and magnitude of a firm's customer relationships are the ultimate means for leveraging business performance. Managing the organization as a portfolio of customers with the purpose of maximizing the value of customer relationships is a formula for both wealth creation and economic growth. For Customer Asset Management to be effective, it is important to recognize that everybody, in one way or another, is an investor. The key to value creation is to see to it that all stakeholders—customer, employees, and shareholders—are treated as investors. There is no mystery about what the investor wants: low risk and high return. That's what the successful company provides. It is also well to remember that economic value is always about the future. The past matters only to the extent that it can be used to predict the future. The greatest value creators are those that predict well. Prediction depends on information. Measurement leads to information. Companies with the best information have a leg up on competition. This may sound obvious, but I have seen too many examples where measurement and information are too disconnected.

The link between customer satisfaction and financial results must be made explicit and continuously updated. There's an infinite number of ways to increase customer satisfaction with zero results on financial results. All satisfaction measurement methods should be calibrated towards financial objectives, or proxies thereof, before they are put into effect. What Best Buy understood early on was that it would be of little value to identify the drivers of customer satisfaction unless these drivers could be linked to internal processes and operations. Otherwise, actions can't be taken and managers cannot be held responsible. In an economy where buyers are getting more powerful at the expense of sellers, good management of customer relationships is becoming an essential ingredient for economic value creation. As buyers become increasingly empowered, investors are going to pay more attention to the quality of a firm's customer relationships. Managers should approach decisions about alternative courses of action with the question: Will the contemplated action strengthen the value of our customer relationships? If the answer is no, the action should not be taken unless there are enough costs savings to offset the depreciation in customer assets. But that would be a rare case.

Notes

CHAPTER 1   INTRODUCTION

1. Pete Blackshaw and Mike Nazzaro, "Consumer Generated Media (CGM) 101 Word of Mouth in the Age of the Web-Fortified Consumer," *Nielsen BuzzMetrics*, 2d ed. (spring 2006).
2. Chris Hart, http://technorati.com/.
3. Claes Fornell, Roland Rust, and Gene Anderson (with E. W. Anderson and R. T. Rust), "Customer Satisfaction, Productivity and Profitability: Differences Between Goods and Services," *Marketing Science* 16:2 (1997): 129–45.
4. Adam Smith, *The Wealth of Nations* (London: Penguin Classics, 1982).
5. Moon Ihlwani and Nichola Saminather, "Hyundai: To Far to Fast? Korea Strong Currency and Costly Moves to Improve Quality are Making its Cars Pricier," *BusinessWeek* (December 2006): 39.
6. Robert Farzad, "A Bigger Voice for Small Investor," *BusinessWeek* (January 2007): 39.
7. Claes Fornell, Sunil Mithas, Forrest V. Morgeson, and M.S. Krishnan, "Customer Satisfaction and Stock Price: High Returns, Low Risk," *Journal of Marketing* (January 2006): 3–14.

CHAPTER 2   THE BIG PICTURE

1. Steven D. Levitt and Stephen J. Dubner, *Freakonomics* (New York: Harper Collins, 2005).

2. Ian Walker, "Wearing a helmet puts cyclists at risk, suggests research," University of Bath press release, September 11, 2006, available at http://www.bath.ac.uk/news/articles/archive/overtaking 110906.html.

3. Clive Thompson, "Cycle Helmets Put You at Risk," *New York Times*, December 10, 2006.

4. Jeremy Siegel and Jeremy Schwartz, "Many Happy Returns," *Wall Street Journal*, March 1, 2007.

5. Phillip J Longman, "The Slowing Pace of Progress," *U.S. News and World Reports*, December 25, 2000.

6. Edward M. Hallowell, *CrazyBusy: Overstretched, Overbooked and About to Snap!* (New York: Ballantine Books, 2006).

7. Source: Bureau of Labor Statistics, http://www.bls.gov/.

8. "Economics and Financial Indicators," *The Economist* 366:8316 (March 20, 2003): 70.

9. Commentary, "Leaders: Power at Last-Crowned at Last, Consumer Power," *The Economist* 375:9 (April 2, 2005).

10. Peter Drucker, *Managing for Results: Economic Tasks and Risk-taking Decisions* (New York: Harper &Row, 1974), 91 1974.

11. Benjamin M. Friedman, *The Moral Consequences of Economic Growth* (New York: Alfred A. Knopf, 2005).

12. The Commerce Department, www.ita.doc.gov/press/publications/ news letters/ita_0207/index.asp February 2007.

13. Mohamed A. El-Erian and Michael Spence, "Capital Currents," *Wall Street Journal*, March 24–25, 2007.

14. David Warsh, *Knowledge and the Wealth of Nations: A Story of Economic Recovery* (New York: W. W. Norton, 2007).

CHAPTER 3   THE SCIENCE OF CUSTOMER SATISFACTION

1. Claes Fornell, "The Science of Satisfaction," *Harvard Business Review* (March 2001): 120–121.

2. Mark Krug, "The Separate Realities of Bush and Kerry Supporters," program on international policy attitudes, University of Maryland, October 21, 2004, available at http://www.counterbias.com/147.html.

3. Robert G. Eccles, "The Performance Measurement Manifesto," *Harvard Business Review* (Jan–Feb 1991): 2–8.

4. Claes Fornell, "Boost Stock Performance, Nation's Economy," *Quality Progress*, (February 2003).

5. Jeremy Bentham, *The Principals of Moral and Legislation* (London 1789).

6. Gregory Berns, *Satisfaction* (New York: Henry Holt and Company, 2005).

7. Peter H. Jacoby, "Sharks Attacks Are A Real Risk to Swimmers," *New York Times* September 9, 2001.

8. Claes Fornell, "A National Customer Satisfaction Barometer: The Swedish Experience," *Journal of Marketing* (1992): 6–21.

9. Peter Achinstein, *Concepts of Science* (Baltimore: Johns Hopkins Press, 1968).

10. Letters to the Public Editor, *New York Times*, April 15, 2007, p. 14.

CHAPTER 4   WHEN CUSTOMER SATISFACTION MATTERS AND WHEN IT DOESN'T

1. Aberdeen Group study cited in Evan Schuman, "Reports Differ on Self-Checkout Value," *eWeek* (October 17, 2006).

2. Federal Communications Commission, 06–179, December 27, 2006, http://hraunfoss.fcc.gov/edocs_public/quickSearch/getResult.

3. Eric Schlosser, *Fast Food Nation* (New York: Harper Perennial, 2005).

4. Wayne F. Cascio, "The High Cost of Low Wages," *Harvard Business Review* (December 2006): 23.
5. Anthony Bianco, *BusinessWeek* (April 30, 2007): 46–56.
6. Vauhini Vara, "Amazon Net Falls Despite Revenue Jump," *Wall Street Journal*, February, 2, 2007.

CHAPTER 5   CUSTOMER SATISFACTION AND STOCK RETURNS: THE POWER OF THE OBVIOUS

1. Claes Fornell, Sunil Mithas, Forrest V. Morgeson, and M.S. Krishnan, "Customer Satisfaction and Stock Prices: High Returns, Low Risk," *Journal of Marketing* 70 (January 2006): 3–14; Eugene W. Anderson, "Customer Satisfaction and Price Tolerance," Marketing letters, & (3), p. 19–30; Eugene W. Anderson, Claes Fornell, and Donald Lehmann, "Customer Satisfaction, Market Share, and Profitability: Findings from Sweden," *Journal of Marketing* 58 (July 1994): 53–66; Eugene W. Andersen, Claes Fornell, and Sanal Mazvacheryl, "Customer Satisfaction and Shareholder Value," *Journal of Marketing* 68 (October 2004): 175–185; Ruth N. Bolton, "A Dynamic Model of the Duration of the Customer's Relationship with Continuous Service Provider: The Role of Satisfaction," *Marketing Science* 17:1 (1998): 45–65; Claes Fornell, "The Science of Satisfaction," *Harvard Business Review* 79 (March 2001): 120–121; C. D. Ittner and D. F. Larcker, "Are Nonfinancial Measures Leading Indicators of Financial Performance? An Analysis of Customer Satisfaction," *Journal of Accounting Reseach* 36 (1998, supplemental): 1–35; C. D. Ittner and D. F. Larcker, *Measuring the Impact of Quality Initiatives on Firm Financial Performance, Advances in the Management of Organizational Quality* (Greenwich, CT: JAI Press, 1996); Roland T. Rust, Christine Moorman, and Peter R. Dickson, "Getting Return

on Quality: Revenue Expansion, Cost Reduction, or Both?" *Journal of Marketing* 66 (2002): 7–24; Sunil Gupta, Donald R Lehmann, and Jennifer Ames Stuart, "Valuing Customer," *Journal of Marketing Research* 41 (February 2004): 7–18; Thomas Gruca and Rego Lupo, "Customer Satisfaction, Cash Flow, and Shareholder Value," *Journal of Marketing* 69 (July 2005): 115–130.

2. Claes Fornell, Michael D. Johnson, Eugene W. Andersen, Jaesung Cha, and Barbara Everitt Bryant, "The American Customer Satisfaction Index: Nature, Purpose and Findings," *Journal of Marketing* 60 (1996): 7–18.

3. Rajendra Srivastava, K. Tasadug, A. Shervani, and Liam Fahey, "Market-Based Assets and Shareholder Value: A Framework for Analysis," *Journal of Marketing* 62 (January 1998): 2–12.

4. "Cell Phone Challenge for Houdini," *New York Times*, March 10, 2007, B1.

5. Burton G. Malkiel, "The Efficient Market Hypothesis and Its Critics," *Journal of Economic Perspectives* 17 (winter 2003): 59–82.

6. Ken Fisher, *The Only Three Questions that Count—Investing by Knowing What Others Don't* (New York: John Wiley & Sons, 2007).

7. *Wall Street Journal*, May 29, 2001.

8. Jonathan B. Berk and Ian Tonks: "Return Persistence and Fund Flows in the Worst Performing Mutual Funds," *National Bureau of Economic Research* (2007).

9. Burton G. Malkiel and Atanu Saha, "Hedge Funds: Risk and Return," *Financial Analysts Journal* 61:6 (2005): 80–88.

10. Jon Hilsenrath, "As Two Economists Debate Markets, the Tide Shifts," *The Wall Street Journal*, October 18, 2004, A1.

11. David Enrich and Jaime Levy Pessin, "Getting Satisfaction," *The Wall Street Journal*, October 14 2006, B3.

12. Claes Fornell, Sunil Mithas, Forrest V. Morgeson, and M.S . Krishnan, "Customer Satisfaction and Stock Prices: High Returns, Low Risk," *Journal of Marketing* 70 (January 2006): 3–14.

13. Patrick McGeehan, "Market Place: Study Questions Advice from Brokerage Firms," *New York Times*, May 29, 2001, C4.
14. Mark Hulbert, "Do Your Homework or Buy an Index Fund," *The New York Times*, April 29, 2007, B5.
15. Sunil Gupta, Donald R, Lehmann, and Jennifer Stuart, "Value Customers," *Journal of Marketing Research* 41 (February 2004): 7–18.
16. C. D. Ittner and D. F. Larcker, "Coming up Short of Non-Financial Performance Measures," *Harvard Business Review* (November 2003), pp. 88–95.

CHAPTER 6   THINGS AREN'T ALWAYS WHAT THEY SEEM: INADVERTENTLY DAMAGING CUSTOMER ASSETS

1. Alex Mindlin, "Please Hold for the Next Available Letdown," *New York Times*, June 25, 2007, p. C4.
2. David Kirkpatrick, "Dell in the Penalty Box: Dell Under Seige," *Fortune*, September 2006, 70.
3. Michael Barbaro, "A Long Line for a Shorter Wait at the Supermarket," *New York Times*, June 23, 2007.
4. Larry Selden and Geoffrey Colvin, "M&A Needn't Be A Loser's Game," *Harvard Business Review*, June 2003, pp. 70–79.

CHAPTER 7   CUSTOMER ASSET MANAGEMENT: OFFENSE VERSUS DEFENSE

1. Sunil Gupta and Donald R. Lehmann, *Managing Customers as Assets: The Strategic Value of Customers in the Long Run* (Philadelphia: Wharton School Publishing, 2005).

2. Julian Villanueva and Dominique Hanssens, "Customer Equity: Measurement, Management and Research Opportunities," *Foundations and Trends in Marketing* 1:7 (2007): 1–95.
3. Letter to shareholders and customers in the AMR Corporation 2001 Annual Report.
4. Al Ehrbar, *Economic Value Added: The Real Key to Creating Wealth* (New York: Wiley Publishing, 1998).

Index